P·R·I·V·A·T·E Obsessions

LEE EZELL

WORD PUBLISHING
Dallas·London·Vancouver·Melbourne

PRIVATE OBSESSIONS: HEALING THE HABITS THAT HAUNT US

Library of Congress Cataloging-in-Publication Data:

Ezell, Lee
    Private obsessions : healing the habits that haunt us / by Lee Ezell.
      p. cm.
    Includes bibliographical references.
    ISBN 0-8499-0903-1
    1. Habit breaking—Religious aspects—Christianity. 2. Compulsive behavior—Religious aspects—Christianity. 3. Christian life—1960-
I. Title.
    BV4598.7.E94 1991
    248.8'6—dc20   91-15150
                                      CIP

Printed in the United States of America

1 2 3 4 5 9 RRD 9 8 7 6 5 4 3 2 1
To all who need a SWORD

*To all who need a SWORD
to slay the DRAGONS—their private obsessions—
that bar the door to
personal peace and joy.*

contents

acknowledgments

Thanks to my "prince of a guy" husband, Hal,
   who patiently waited out my obsession with this book.

Thanks to my three daughters, Pamela, Sandra, and Julie,
   who still claim me in spite of my compulsive behavior.

Thanks to Lela Gilbert, an excellent journalist and friend,
   who addictively worked on unscrambling this manuscript.

before

I thought long and hard before writing this book on obsessive, compulsive, and addictive behavior. I wrestled with whether or not I was qualified to write it, although I perceived a great need for it.

No, this author has never been a drug addict, an alcoholic, nor a husband abuser (well, one out of three isn't bad). But I realized that if just being compulsive would qualify me, I've done my graduate work in the field. The Broadway tune, "I'm just a girl who can't say no," fits me to a tee.

I even lay awake at night, imagining my mother's being interviewed about my writing this book:

> Well, my daughter Lee was really never much of a writer. She could talk good, but write? No. A good daughter who is a writer would write her own mother a letter now and then . . .
>
> So now she's writing a book about addiction? At last, something she knows about! When Lee was a health-food nut, she bugged me about vitamins. When she was a religious addict, she'd try to get me "saved." When Lee was workaholic, she was too busy to call her mother (even though I gave her the best years of my life . . .).

For many months I have been addictively working on this manuscript. I have been obsessed with its need to be comprehensive, and I have compulsively sought answers. I imagined what my compulsive readers would say:

- "It gave me a real high!"
- "I just gobbled it up!"
- "I've already bought eight copies, and now I'm going back for more!"

- "It consumed me. It was all I thought about. I just couldn't put it down."
- "I have to have the sequel—now."
- "I'll take odds on its success."

The point is, you don't have to be an alcoholic or a drug addict to have a problem with obsessive thoughts, compulsive behavior, or addictive habits. Many of us look to other more "acceptable" behavior (napping, eating, shopping, working) to achieve the same goal of "feeling better" or escaping pain. I know. In many ways, I "wrote the book" on compulsive behavior—long before I got around to writing a book. But I have learned some things about how such thoughts, behaviors, and habits can be overcome, and I do want to share them with you.

This book, then, is a conglomeration of what I have struggled with, experienced, counseled, observed, and re-searched. It's not intended to be a clinical analysis of the topic or a substitute for professional therapy in the case of severe addictions. Instead, this text and the exercises contained within were designed as an upbeat self-therapy, based on spiritual principles, to enable ordinary readers to purge their lives from the hindrance of obsessive, compulsive, addictive behavior. I urge you to allow this reading to assist you to identify, develop, and practice therapeutic skills for overcoming compulsive behavior.

Through the preparation of this book I've come to analyze my own personal "little foxes" that were spoiling my "vines."[1] I'm coming to a freedom I've never known. The text which follows is intended to lead readers past their private obsessions and into true personal freedom!

---

1. Song of Solomon 2:15.

do you have a private obsession?

1

---

smart women, dumb behavior

do you have a private obsession?

VANESSA

Her wind-tossed hair glistening gold and brown in the afternoon sunlight, Vanessa slammed the front door and rushed toward the car. She would just make it on time to a five o'clock meeting with a client, and she couldn't afford to be late. She was a professional, after all. Besides, this was the third time her client had looked at the Martin property. Vanessa was almost positive he would be making an offer. If he did, if it was accepted, *and* if escrow closed, she would pocket a neat fifteen thousand dollars.

Others might have prayed. Vanessa simply crossed her fingers, took a deep breath, and screeched out of the driveway, leaving her son Jason in front of his TV playing Super Mario Brothers®.

"It's just as well . . ." she thought with a twinge of guilt that he'd been playing video games all day. "At least he won't be out in the street where he can get into trouble. And he's going to his father's this weekend; they'll probably go to the beach or something. Besides, if I clinch this deal, I can make it up to him next week. . . ."

At the traffic light around the corner, Vanessa stole a look
in the rear-view mirror and smiled at the oblong slice of face
that smiled back at her. Not bad at all—she looked a decade
younger than her forty-one years. And her looks were no
accident. Despite her frantic schedule, she almost never
missed her tennis dates or health-club workouts—a day or two
without exercise and she was a nervous wreck. And she hadn't
tasted sugar in a couple of years—she was afraid if she ever
let go and got off her diet she would blow up like a balloon in
a matter of weeks.

Vanessa was determined not to let herself go. She had made
that vow when Gerald had left her—she'd show him what he
was missing. And it worked. Although her life since the
divorce had been a jigsaw of male relationships and nothing
permanent had evolved, she rarely lacked for dates. And now
there was Chad. . . .

"Wait till I tell Chad about the sale!" she giggled to herself.
"Better yet, I won't tell him. I'll just show up in my new BMW®,
and he can draw his own conclusions!" Impressing her new
heartthrob with a fabulous car made the sale of the Barker
house all the more appealing. The fifteen-hundred-dollar
down payment would be well spent if it could contribute to a
more satisfying friendship with her elusive land-developer
friend.

A wave of uncertainty fluttered within her as she drove a
little too fast toward her Century 21® office. Jason needed
braces—no question about it. And Hilary wanted to be involved in an exchange-student program, which could easily
cost several thousand dollars. Vanessa desperately wanted the
BMW, but what about Jason's teeth? Worse yet, what would
her fourteen-year-old daughter say?

"Dad's right about you, Mom. You are *totally* selfish. . . ."
She could hear it all now!

"Those kids!" Vanessa muttered, her momentary elation
drowned by doubt and fear. "I haven't even sold the property
yet, and I'm already feeling guilty about how I'm going to
spend the money!"

She burst through the office entrance. "Any messages?" she
asked the receptionist hopefully. Maybe Chad had called.

"No, nothing so far. . . ." Vaguely disappointed, Vanessa glanced at her watch. Did she have time to call Chad just to let him know where she was? Better not. She didn't want to seem too anxious.

Checking to see if her client was waiting, she dashed back toward the bathroom. Closing the door, she did a few stretches, trying to shrug out the tension in her shoulders. After this appointment, maybe she would have time to run by the club. A run or a couple of sets of tennis was just what she needed. Instinctively calmer, Vanessa assessed herself in the mirror, brushed her hair, glossed her lips, and straightened the lapels of her Liz Claiborne® blazer. Then, drawing a long breath, she slowly made her way toward her desk. When her client walked through the office door, she was waiting, well composed, and smiling warmly.

DEBI

The door closed decisively, and Debi listened for Dennis's car to start. Then she yawned as she turned back to the newspaper that was unfolded in front of her. Another day. . . . She stifled another yawn as she sipped a cup of steaming Cinnamon Mist herb tea and scanned the astrological forecast.

"Virgo: Good timing for you to explore that new vision. Don't be afraid! Intriguing opportunities lie ahead."

A surge of excitement tingled within her, and the familiar feeling of vague dissatisfaction retreated. She jumped up, and ran into the bedroom. Her bright blue eyes sparkled back at her from the looking glass as she quickly brushed on her makeup. She glanced momentarily at the wedding picture proudly displayed on the chest of drawers. A fabulously attractive couple smiled at her—Dennis and Debi—married just a year before.

"That was *then*. This is *now!*" She rummaged through a drawer until she found a handful of plastic credit cards Dennis had "hidden" there and stuffed them into her handbag. Dennis would never know if she bought herself a few little items at the Fashion Plaza's grand opening. After all, hadn't her horoscope told her to "explore the new vision?"

Besides, a petulant little voice argued inside her head, Dennis never noticed anything she did, anyway . . .

Debi had always been the center of attention in high school and college. Her all-American good looks and her bubbly personality had kept her involved in every kind of activity. And of course, she'd married her sweetheart, Dennis, captain of the football team, president of the student body. The wedding, as witnessed by the portrait, had been a production.

But now? She could hardly believe it herself, but Dennis was, well, her resident couch potato. He watched his sports. He read his paper. He listened to his music. Meanwhile, friends no longer surrounded Debi. Studies and wedding preparations no longer kept her occupied. For some reason Dennis didn't want her to work, and decorating the house had quickly become a bore. So Debbie shopped. And searched for meaning. She filled her life with new, fascinating facts about herself that she learned from her yoga teacher, her horoscope, and the women's pop-psych books she read continuously.

Before leaving the house for the mall, Debi quietly walked across the bedroom to a small table and picked up a sparkling piece of crystal. She held it in her hands, closed her eyes, and breathed deeply, listening intently for an inner voice that just might give her more guidance for the day.

"Color . . ." was what she thought she heard in her mind. That glimpse of insight tied in perfectly with what she already had decided. "Brighten your world with color. . . ." The thought stayed with her as she closed the garage down and backed out of the driveway.

Once in the mall, Debi stifled a small surge of guilt. Dennis would be furious. And she really didn't need any more stuff. "But I won't buy all that much," she told herself. "I just need to get out of the house. And I have been needing a new leotard—something bright. . . . Color—that's it."

By day's end Debi had explored her new vision. She'd brightened her world with color. She'd gotten out of the house. And she'd managed to spend five hundred dollars she and Dennis really didn't have.

IS THIS BOOK FOR YOU?

Fortunately, Vanessa and Debi have never met. And they would have next-to-nothing in common if they found themselves in an unexpected conversation somewhere. But they share something that neither of them even recognizes. Both these women—like many others—suffer from what I call private obsessions. Some people call them hidden addictions. Whatever you call the problem, these people have come to depend on certain activities to keep from feeling bored, depressed, or anxious.

Vanessa is hooked on male/female relationships, physical fitness, and power. Debi is fascinated with New-Age phenomena and can't resist credit cards. And neither one is really in control of her thoughts and habits.

Does any of this sound familiar?

"Oh, yeah, that reminds me of _____," you may say. Or maybe (perish the thought) it sounds a little like you, too.

If either statement applies, read on!

Jack Henningfield of the National Institute on Drug Abuse reports in *Newsweek* magazine, "Anyone with a healthy, functioning nervous system is vulnerable to addiction."[1]

That leaves room for all of us, doesn't it? Did you ever think of yourself as an addict? Probably not. But have you ever:

- sought freedom from a personal habit that has the power to get out of control?
- struggled with low self-esteem and felt that some negative habit or another was justified?
- imagined that only "drug addicts" have a life-sapping problem, and yet couldn't seem to stop doing some "small" thing or other?
- felt short-changed in the self-discipline category or lacked the willpower to control a nagging habit?

If so, you might just be a small-time addict. But don't feel alone—and don't despair! Thousands of women suffer from

---

1. Jack Henningfield, "Roots of Addiction," *Newsweek,* 2 February 1989, 53.

private obsessions. And thousands have found help and healing for their problems. I hope this book will help you as well.

But first of all, a few words about what this book is *not*. It is not a reference book on addiction. And it is *not* for:

- anyone who is chemically addicted to drugs, illegal or prescriptive,
- anyone who is addicted to alcohol,
- anyone who has a life-threatening addiction of any kind,
- sufferers of OCD (Obsessive/Compulsive Disorder), or any other illness which involves abnormal activity in certain regions of the brain,
- anyone displaying seriously crippling behavior such as agoraphobia, kleptomania, or the like.

Instead, it is an offering for those plagued with habits they are beginning to recognize as affecting their quality of life and wish to stop. Maybe—just maybe—it's a book for you.

AN ADDICTED SOCIETY?

We live in a strange world—one that almost seems to encourage addiction of one sort or another. In our Western society, for instance, it seems that no one can be too thin, too fit, or work too hard at looking great. No wonder some people develop fixations with diet, exercise, and appearance! Our culture also seems to reward overwork and material acquisition, feeding our tendency to become workaholics, "shopaholics"—even compulsive coupon clippers. And the stress of our fast-paced lifestyle tempts all of us to seek solace in comforting substances and behavior—from caffeine and television to alcohol and cocaine.

True, alcohol, drugs, and tobacco seem to be losing some of the glamour they once enjoyed. In fact, "recovery" from addiction almost seems to be the "chic" thing nowadays. To read the media accounts, you would think that all the "beautiful people" are busy "getting straight." They are out and about each night at their therapy groups, still paying for their trip to the Betty Ford Center and the follow-up time they spent at the Schick Center—the "temple of getting straight, the Shangri-La of sobriety." They publicly confess their glamorous shortcomings and earnestly report on their progress. Some of them even seem hooked on the process of getting better. (Is it possible they've traded one form of compulsion for another?)

Outside of the spotlight, a lot of individuals are busy nursing their private obsessions, habits well hidden from the public eye. And they're thinking, "Thank God I don't have a problem like *those* addicts do!" Habits plague them, but they are not life-threatening, so they are hurting no one but themselves. Well, yes, maybe their behavior tends to sap their spiritual strength and self-image. But not to worry—they can handle it.

Or can they?

As thousands of people around the country will testify, getting "unhooked" just isn't that easy. But before we get into *why*, let's look a little more closely at what addiction is and how it develops.

THE MANY FACES OF ADDICTION

An *addiction* is any repeated need or habit over which we are powerless. It takes control of us, causing us to do and think things that are inconsistent with our own personal values.

Anyone caught in the addictive process has a strong conscious desire or need for something—a substance, a fantasy, an action, or an atmosphere that produces a physical and/or mental "high" or a relief from anxiety. It thus offers an escape from physical or emotional discomfort or pressure.

Years ago addictions were viewed as a social problem or forms of criminal behavior. Modern thinking now identifies addiction as a disease. This "disease" may include not only dependency-forming substances (such as caffeine and nicotine, alcohol and drugs), but a looser collection of activities including excessive gambling, eating, TV watching, and similar habits. It covers a continuum from mild addictions (those that are not really dangerous in themselves, but that

could develop into serious problems) to severe addictions
(those that seriously threaten health or relationships).

   Generally, addictions fall into two categories:

> **Substance Addictions**
>
> **and**
>
> **Process Addictions**

   The *substance addict* is dependent on a drug of some sort,
legal or illegal. This could include prescription drugs, alcohol,
or cocaine, as well as nicotine or even certain foods—anything taken into the body's chemistry. A substance addiction
involves a *physical dependency* on the addictive substance.

   A *process addict* demonstrates a behavioral habit or dependence on an activity or relationship. Process addictions include being an overpowering parent, an entertainment junkie,
a pack rat, a music junkie, and countless others. The private
obsessions that are the subject of this book are process addictions.

   The line between these two kinds of dependencies is sometimes blurred. For example, research has shown that some
drug addicts who "mainline" drugs (inject them in veins)
become hooked on the process of "shooting up" as well as on
the drug itself.

   And other experts, including Christian psychologist
Archibald Hart, believe many process addictions have a basis
in brain chemistry. For instance, workaholics may become
physically "hooked" on the rush of adrenalin they get from
pushing themselves to the limit.[2]

   But even though not all addictions fall easily into the two
cate-gories (food addictions are particularly tricky), the
distinction between substance addictions and process addictions can be helpful.

----

   2. Archibald D. Hart, *Healing Life's Hidden Addictions: Overcoming
the Closet Compulsions That Waste Your Time and Control Your Life* (Ann
Arbor: Servant Publications, 1990) and Hart, *Adrenalin and Stress* (Waco,
TX: Word, 1988).

IT ALL BEGINS IN THE MIND

You may be wondering why this book is called *Private Obsessions* if it's really about addictions. That's because *obsessions* refers to what happens in the mind—and that's where addictions begin.

Actually, the terms *addiction, obsession,* and *compulsion* are very closely related, and I will sometimes use them interchangeably. (After all, this book is supposed to be a down-to-earth self-help book, not a clinical textbook.) But there are a few distinctions between the terms that can be helpful to know.[3]

An *obsession,* basically, is a thought or idea which dominates our thinking. An addiction may start with obsessive thoughts about something. And once an addiction is established—especially when we try to break it—it tends to dominate our thoughts.

The term *compulsion* refers to actions. It describes behavior that we feel "driven" or "compelled" to carry out—whether it is drinking, eating, cleaning, or reading. It is the compulsive character of a behavior that determines whether it is harmless or beneficial or addictive and enslaving. Any "good" action can become unhealthy when it becomes compulsive. All addictions involve compulsive behavior.

Sometimes, compulsive behavior can result from *unconscious* thoughts—we don't really know where our action comes from. But if the compulsive action is repeated, chances are a conscious obsessive thought process will then develop. So the two almost always go hand in hand.

In actual practice, obsessions and compulsions are related to the *addictive process.* A repeated pattern of obsessive thoughts and compulsive behavior can lead to an addiction, and an addiction in turn causes obsessive thoughts and compulsive behavior.

In actual practice, obsessions and compulsions are related to the *addictive process.* A repeated pattern of obsessive thoughts and compulsive behavior can lead to an addiction, and an addiction in turn causes obsessive thoughts and compulsive behavior.

---

3. Once again, I am using the terms in their more general sense and am not referring to the clinical anxiety condition called Obsessive-Compulsive Disorder, which sometimes triggers similar behavior but is a very different problem.

Say, for instance, that a woman feels the temptation to chat (again) with a friend. (Her dilemma is illustrated in figure 1.) She knows that another conversation would both stimulate and tranquilize her; she's the type that finds her adventure in "romancing the phone." Each time this woman gives in to her temptation, she is paving a habitual escape route—via AT&T—and eventually she is "hooked." Even though she may try to restrain herself, all she can think about is the phone (she's *obsessed* with it). She feels as if something were "pushing" her to make that phone call (calling has become a *compulsion*). Her temptation has become a habitual need *(she's addicted)*.

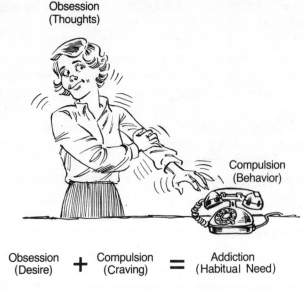

Obsession
(Thoughts)

Compulsion
(Behavior)

Obsession		Compulsion		Addiction
(Desire)	**+**	(Craving)	**=**	(Habitual Need)

Figure 1

Obsessive thoughts and compulsive actions are not impossible to stop (although they sometimes seem that way). But they do become progressively harder to resist as the addiction process proceeds.

Every private obsession begins with a simple thought—a desire or temptation. It is at that point that we determine whether or not they are "right" or "good," judging by the measure of the highest good of which our conscience is aware. And at that point we can choose whether to feed or starve the thought. If we feed it, it can easily progress from simple thought to obsessive thought, compulsive action, and even addiction. And as the patterns of thought and action become "burned in" to our habit patterns, they move past the point where they can be easily controlled.

Suppose, for instance, a married woman thinks about flirting with a man (not her husband—she's already bagged him). Her conscience will automatically register whether or not this is "OK" for her to do, judging by the highest standard she has accepted for herself. At this point, in the thought stage, she can choose whether to dismiss the thought or think about it some more. Thus a passing thought has the potential to become a thriving obsession, ready to blossom into a compulsive action or, eventually, a full-blown addiction. And putting a stop to obsessive thoughts, compulsive actions, and hidden addictions is much more difficult than stopping a thought the first time it occurs.

THE HABIT COMPLICATION

I have said that an addiction—hidden or not—is essentially a habit. And that is one important reason that private obsessions are so hard to stop.

Any skill we've ever learned and practiced becomes a habit—typing, putting on makeup, driving a car—we do them all by habit. We learn to function "on automatic pilot" without even thinking about what we're doing. And that's good. It's a God-given function of our bodies and minds that saves us time and energy.

The problem, of course, is that our nervous systems cannot distinguish between useful behaviors and dangerous ones. Any repeated behavior—healthy or unhealthy—can develop into a habit. In a sense, then, being healed from hidden addictions means breaking old, unhealthy habits and developing new, healthy ones in their place. Self-control really means establishing a new habit pattern. All recovery demands change—the changing of our habits.

Be prepared, however, for a private battle!

> **Change**
> **is a**
> **civil war!**

Believe me, I know . . .

LEE'S CONFESSION

It's 10:15 A.M., and my mouth is beginning to water.
"Sugar! Sugar!" something cries out from within and, like a
robot, I stray toward the donut box at work. A rich, sticky
chocolate-iced creation finds its way into my hand.
   "It's not that I want it," I tell myself. "I need it in order to
work through the morning effectively." I need that boost, that
little shot of sugar. The craving is justified.
   Same thing again, only now it's summertime and I'm
sitting in my car at a traffic light, minding my own business.
It's that hungry time of the afternoon—3:15. The grocery bags
are on the back seat, and in them is a large, economy-sized
bag of M&Ms®, which suddenly begins to sing to me. I reach
over the seat and pull the M&Ms bag to the front seat with
me. "Just a handful," I tell myself as I turn up the radio.
   Seven handfuls later, I have chocolate on the steering wheel
(the milk chocolate *did* melt in my hands!). But somehow the
"crunch" has its grip on me again, and I'm unconsciously
doing what I told myself I would *not* do—munching another
handful of M&Ms.
   Now I'm reasoning and arguing with myself as I drive.
"This will be the last mouthful. . . . But, then, I've already
done this much damage, so I might as well eat till I get home.
Then I can hide the bag!
   Suddenly a small voice cries out from within, "STOP!"
Quickly I pull over to the curb—real fast before I can change
my mind again. I grab the bag of temptations, jump out of the
car and slam them into the trunk!
   No big deal? Maybe you don't think so. But I do.
   Like you, I'm a person who has not escaped the crippling
power of addictions myself. Working. TV. Shopping. Yes, I'm

also a chocoholic.

Self-control has never been my strong suit—I'm an outgoing (some might say flighty), "sanguine" type of personality who tends to be more interested in having fun than in controlling anything. When it comes to food, like I tell my friends "I have no problem with being twenty pounds overweight. I refuse to be a slave to willpower!" Seriously, I have carefully taught myself never to say the naughty "D" word— *discipline*. I am a world-class procrastinator (my husband will testify to that). And I am the kind of person who resists taking time for self-analysis (it's too dull).

But I'm learning. Though my personal "gremlins" are not publicly disabling, I have attempted to identify them and am in the process of becoming free of their power through the principles set forth in this book. I have finally recognized my personal addictions. I have admitted to myself that they were robbing my life of precious moments and filling me with frustration. And I have begun the process of breaking free.

IT'S NOT JUST A MATTER OF WILLPOWER

So, what about you? Is there a chance that you might have a gremlin or two yourself? Are you willing, at least, to consider the possibility? If so, why not take a stab at Self-Test #1? This inventory is designed to enable you to pinpoint a problem area. And, while you're at it, why not check out the list of potentially harmful behavior patterns beginning on page 49. You may see some familiar habits there. And once you recognize the problem, you will be on your way toward finding freedom.

But as anyone who has struggled with a bad habit knows, it won't be easy.

Breaking free from obsessive thoughts, compulsive behavior, and any kind of addiction requires more than self-generated effort. Freedom is based on something more than "turning over a new leaf" or "pulling ourselves up by our bootstraps." We need a grace beyond ourselves. Fortunately, as thousands of recovering people have discovered, that grace is readily available to us, if we open ourselves up to it.

This book, therefore, is about *willingness* . . . not about *will-power*. It is based on the assumption that all of us, at times, are bothered by some behavior that we are powerless to control. Are you willing to take the chance that you fit into that category?

Maybe the title *Private Obsessions* seems a little too potent for you. You may not have such a life-threatening habit as drug or alcohol addition. Be thankful you don't! And you may be functioning just fine. And yet . . .

Although you may not be on the verge of a blow-out, you're wearing a bit thin. You have a slow leak. Maybe no one would describe you as "hooked," an "addict," or a "junkie," but you are well aware of that one bad habit in your life. You consider it your "bent," your "one vice," a small blemish on your character.

Guess what? If you cannot control that behavior, if it is controlling you, you are an addict. You have a private obsession, however small you may perceive it to be. Not only will it not be "manicured" away. It also has the potential and the propensity to grow—and it's hard to shake.

Chances are, of course, that you're not totally in the dark about what your private obsession is. In fact, you may have tried many times, without success, to overcome it.

In fact, whether the struggle is with sweets, with overuse of credit cards, a compulsion to exercise, or any other hard-to-shake habit, most people with private obsessions suffer from:

- an occasional or periodic sense of despair,
- insufficient willpower to overcome,
- a sense that the remedy is "out of reach."

No question about it—we need more than willpower alone to overcome private obsessions and hidden addictions. And there is no easy, magic formula for success. You'll not hear me saying "All you have to do is this and bingo, you're cured!" It's not that simple.

In fact, the solutions presented in this book are not a *plan*. They represent something far more significant than a quick formula for change. They are a pattern for thinking. A point of view.

But they work. In fact, they are changing my life.

I hope they can help you as well.

self-test #1
do you have a private obsession?

Check below anything that dominates your thoughts or actions, that you feel deprived if forced to give up, and/or that is causing you stress:

_____ Abstaining from food
_____ Achievement/success
_____ Airing my problems
_____ Analyzing my thoughts and emotions
_____ Analyzing the thoughts and emotions of others
_____ Attending church and church-related meetings
_____ Attending seminars/conferences
_____ Bargain hunting
_____ Being "in fashion"/trendy
_____ Being a Supermom
_____ Being seen/heard
_____ Bingeing on food
_____ Clipping coupons
_____ Collecting/hobbies
_____ Dieting
_____ Doing things "right"
_____ Eating or drinking substances with caffeine or sugar
_____ Fear(s)
_____ Gathering information
_____ Gathering professional advice
_____ Having music in background
_____ Individual therapy
_____ Keeping surroundings immaculate
_____ Keeping up with the Joneses
_____ Keeping up to the minute with news events
_____ Maintenance of pet(s)
_____ Making everything perfect
_____ Making money

_____ Meeting others' needs
_____ Meeting the "right one"
_____ My horoscope predictions
_____ My next meal
_____ Napping or resting
_____ Negative qualities of child(ren)
_____ Nutrition
_____ Orderliness/cleanliness
_____ Participating in sports activities
_____ Physical health
_____ Physical fitness
_____ Physical thrills
_____ Pleasing people
_____ Pornographic material
_____ Positive qualities of child(ren)
_____ Reading popular novels (or other favorite reading
         material)
_____ Relationship with the opposite sex
_____ Religious "dos and don'ts"
_____ Risky relationships
_____ Romantic feelings
_____ Saving money
_____ Saving the world
_____ Scheduling meals (and staying on schedule)
_____ Seeking the "unknown"
_____ Serving others
_____ Sexual fantasies
_____ Shopping
_____ Support groups
_____ Talking on the telephone
_____ Television soaps (updates)
_____ The shape I am (figure)
_____ The shape I'm in (exercise)
_____ Viewing sporting events
_____ Volunteering
_____ What I'm going to eat next
         Other: Fill in the blank:

_____   _____
_____   _____

Keeping the above checklist in mind and referring to your possible private obsession as "IT," answer the following questions as honestly as you can:

1. Can IT wait? _____ Yes _____ No

2. Has IT moved beyond a *want* to a *need*?
   _____ Yes _____ No

3. Is IT interfering with my everyday living?
   _____ Yes _____ No

4. Do I schedule my time and activities to revolve around IT?
   _____ Yes _____ No

5. Does IT dominate my thoughts? _____ Yes _____ No

6. Do I find myself doing IT when I don't really want to?
   _____ Yes _____ No

7. Is IT becoming too much of a priority?
   _____ Yes _____ No

8. Does IT disrupt my home life? _____ Yes _____ No

9. Is IT causing me problems with my family or friends?
   _____ Yes _____ No

10. Does IT cause me to neglect my important relationships?
    _____ Yes _____ No

11. Has IT ever gotten me into financial trouble?
    _____ Yes _____ No

12. Is IT detrimental to my life's work? _____ Yes _____ No

13. Has my efficiency in various areas of my life decreased because of IT? _____ Yes _____ No

14. Is IT potentially hazardous to my health?
    _____ Yes _____ No

15. Does IT affect my ability to rest? _____ Yes _____ No

16. When I cannot have IT, do I feel deprived?
    _____ Yes _____ No

17. Do I find myself covering IT up or denying IT?
    ____ Yes ____ No

18. Have I ever lied about IT? ____ Yes ____ No

19. Have people who love me expressed concern about IT?
    ____ Yes ____ No

20. Am I irritated when someone brings IT up or wants to talk about IT? ____ Yes ____ No

21. Do I fear someone will discover IT? ____ Yes ____ No

22. Does IT give me a sense of well-being and stability?
    ____ Yes ____ No

23. Does IT make me feel I am out of control of my life?
    ____ Yes ____ No

24. Does IT ever cause me to break my personal code of ethics or morals? ____ Yes ____ No

25. Do I feel guilty after engaging in IT?
    ____ Yes ____ No

26. Have I lost respect for myself because of IT?
    ____ Yes ____ No

27. Do I engage in IT to escape worry or trouble—or just to "feel better"? ____ Yes ____ No

28. Do I engage in IT to boost my self-confidence?
    ____ Yes ____ No

29. Do I feel insecure about IT? ____ Yes ____ No

30. Is IT the last thing in the world I want to talk about?
    ____ Yes ____ No

31. Do I find myself blaming IT on others—"It's not my fault; you made me!"? ____ Yes ____ No

32. Am I angry I cannot stop IT? ____ Yes ____ No

33. Have I noticed ITs frequency increasing?
    ____ Yes ____ No

34. Do I know IT is detrimental or destructive and yet continue IT? ____ Yes ____ No

35. Am I afraid IT has control over me? ____ Yes ____ No

36. Have I failed to keep my promises about keeping IT under control or cutting down? ____ Yes ____ No

37. Do I think about changing IT, but avoid any actual commitment? ____ Yes ____ No

38. Do I doubt I could change IT even if I wanted to? ____ Yes ____ No

39. Do I feel a need to change IT? ____ Yes ____ No

40. Is IT something I long to be free from? ____ Yes ____ No

Now go back and count your "yes" answers:

- *If you answered "yes" to 12 or more questions, you most likely have a private obsession.*
- *If you answered "yes" to 8-11 questions, watch out; you may be well on your way toward having a private obsession.*
- *If you answered "yes" to 4-7 questions, you may have the potential to have a private obsession.*
- *If you answered "yes" to 3 or fewer questions, you are probably not in danger of developing a private obsession in the near future.*

Having identified the things that dominate my thoughts or actions and/or are causing me stress, and having honestly answered the above questions and scored myself, I believe I have (or could have) a private obsession with

_____.

2

---

so that's why they call it a "fix"!

understanding your private obsessions

I commend you for getting this far! It should be an encouraging sign to you that you're ready for a new lease on life. You have a desire to examine yourself, to face facts, to be different. And that's exciting!

Keep in mind, however, that the following statement was never more true than when it is applied to the area of private obsessions:

> one can never be mistaken
> in pointing out that issues are always
> more complicated than
> we want them to be,
> more complicated than we can address
> in one book or one sermon,
> even more complicated
> than we can fully understand

Yes, we are complex people. Yet, in spite of the very real complications, let's commit ourselves to self-examination and learn a bit more about what makes us think, feel, and act the way we do—with true inner freedom as our ultimate goal. And just so we know we're not in this alone, let's meet a couple more women with their own private obsessions.

SARAH

Sarah was energetically scrubbing the kitchen counter when the phone rang . . . again.

"Darn!" She spat the word out so angrily that it almost sounded like profanity. This was the third phone call in an hour, and her cleaning was way behind schedule.

"Hello?" The irritation showed in her voice. She had been asked by her church to coordinate a used clothing drive, and how she wished she'd said no! Emmanuel Methodist Church was a second home to Sarah, and sixty-year-old Sarah was always deeply concerned about the many social issues her pastors embraced. But this one was clearly an inconvenience.

"A couch and chair? No, I'm sorry, we are only interested in clothing for the Indian reservation. No! I have no idea. Why don't you call Goodwill? No, we do not pick up. You'll have to bring it to the church yourself. . . ." Her response was crisp. This was the second time a contributor had misunderstood the rather nebulous announcement in the church bulletin. Sarah had been left to answer too many unnecessary questions.

Muttering to herself, Sarah hung up the phone, then impulsively took it off the hook. She exchanged the Fantastic® spray bottle for the clear blue Windex® and got back to work.

It was Tuesday, and, despite the interruptions, Sarah's kitchen was beginning to gleam. Monday brought clean laundry, Wednesday was for bathrooms, Thursday dusting and vacuuming, and Friday—always a favorite—was baking day. Saturday Sarah worked in the garden, and in the afternoon she entertained some of her acquaintances from church. And Sunday was, well, *Sunday*. Church, for Sarah, was a deeply satisfying institution. Although its spiritual dimensions eluded her, she had always practiced Judeo-Christian morality, and the small congregation of Emmanuel members provided her with all the social life she could ever want.

Sarah's world revolved around her church activities. She was always the first to bring cookies and cakes to the bake sales—always the most delectable sweets imaginable—and was happy to sit outside after services gathering signatures for the various political petitions Rev. MacNeill circulated regularly. These tasks did not interfere with Sarah's daily schedule of cleaning house, marketing, going to the post office, and preparing her simple meals.

If only she hadn't been foolish enough to get involved in this miserable clothing drive! Determined to make up for lost time, she worked twice as fast. As it was, she'd be late preparing and eating her dinner. Would the dishes and kitchen be cleaned up in time for the seven o'clock news?

"Tomorrow I'm having a word with Rev. MacNeill about his secretary," Sarah grumbled to herself. "Why can't that young woman get things straight in the bulletin? That's her job! Maybe he ought to find one who can. . . ."

With that, brushing a loose strand of gray hair out of her eyes, Sarah put away the Windex® and pulled out the cookbook. Even though she'd been widowed for ten years, she still maintained the habit of preparing a "good, well-balanced meal" every night. Where was that quickie chicken teriyaki recipe, anyway? If she could make it work for the chicken she'd thawed, she just might get herself back on schedule!

CLARICE

Clarice pumped her arms harder as she strode around the corner toward her house, breathing heavily. Then she reached up to adjust the volume on her headphones so that Pastor Jack Hayford's sermon would not be lost in the traffic noise. Although she was nearly fifty pounds overweight, Clarice made a point of exercising regularly. After all, her body was the temple of God, wasn't it? And even if she was a little overweight, there was no reason she should let herself go.

"Right on!" she responded to a biblical point that appealed to her. Pastor Jack was always right on, and she was thankful that technology made it possible for her to jog with him every morning.

Clarice unlocked her door and went into the kitchen. Before she plugged in the coffee pot, she flipped on the cassette player. A praise tape soon filled the house with music. "Thank the Lord the kids are back in school. Now I can spend some time with Him alone!" She checked the clock and felt a momentary twinge of anxiety. She'd promised Bud she would pick up his coat from the cleaner's before they closed, and the library committee was still waiting on her report. But those things would have to wait. Dr. Dobson's broadcast was about to begin, and she didn't want to miss it.

Clarice reached for a hidden package of sweet rolls and pulled herself off an ample portion. Her heart was still pumping from the recent exertion, and she collapsed into a chair, humming along with the tape as she savored the hot coffee and the cherry-and-cheese Danish. Fortunately for her, the kids hadn't found it first!

Clarice was happier these days, or comparably so. Her husband, Bud, who was what most of her Bible teachers described as a "carnal" Christian, had been thoroughly disgusted with her size for years. He was quick to compare her with slimmer, shapelier women. And though she had explained to him that she was big-boned and really didn't eat that much, he just snorted. So she had spent the last twenty years on one diet after another. All of them had worked—but not for long.

Now, just recently, a Christian radio talk show had explained it all to her. "There's something deep in your past, dear," the kindly host had responded to her phoned-in question. "It's buried more deeply than you know. Oh, yes, Jesus can help you. You don't need another diet. You need emotional healing—a lot of it. It's understandable that you are overeating; you're just giving yourself a little pleasure to compensate for the pain of the past."

Clarice had felt a burden of guilt lift that very day. She had felt a new freedom. Unfortunately, she'd gained fifteen pounds in the weeks that followed. But at least she could see why her weight problem was so persistent. Maybe she did overeat—a little—but there was a reason.

"So what if I'm overweight? So what if Bud says I'm thinking too much about myself? He's concerned too much with the external, anyway. God knows I can't help being big. He knows why I'm 'me.' I need to learn to love myself so I can love God and my family better. I've been a 'pleaser' long enough. It's time Bud and the kids pleased me for a change!" And she helped herself to another sweet roll as she turned off the music and tuned in Dr. Dobson.

TOO MUCH OF A GOOD THING

Sarah and Clarice, like Vanessa and Debi, are addicts. Sarah is a slave to her schedule and a workaholic around her house. Clarice is a compulsive eater who is also hooked on religious pop-psych. And Sarah's and Clarice's stories point out several important characteristics of private obsessions:

(1) *Good things—even religion—can become the objects of private obsessions.* Certainly there is nothing bad about clean houses and disciplined schedules and good food and personal growth! But these ladies have carried their "good" commitments to extremes and are becoming self-centered and overindulgent because of them.

Religious people, furthermore—even dedicated Christians—are not exempt from private obsessions—even "religious addictions." *Any* thought or behavior—good or bad, religious or profane—can become the stuff of addiction.

(2) *Private obsessions almost always involve denial.* Both Sarah and Clarice would deny that they have a problem. Oh, Sarah is aware that people are bothering her, and Clarice knows she is overweight! But neither one is thinking very clearly about the relationship between their feelings and their actions. And neither one would admit—to herself or to anyone else—that she is hooked.

What's worse, both Sarah and Clarice are using the "good" nature of their activities to fuel their denial. "We're good, responsible, Christian people—not addicts," they would say if challenged. "We don't have those sort of troubles in our church" is too often the reply of religious people when talking about addictions. But deny as we may, no one group of human beings is exempt from temptation when it comes to private obsessions.

(3) *Private obsessions often travel in "packs."* In other words, it is not uncommon for people to develop more than one private obsession. We saw this with Vanessa and Debi, too. And it's even true of substance addictions. Addicts of any kind easily develop "cross addictions" to other things or people.

(4) *Private obsessions involve an attempt to "fix" unpleasant feelings instead of facing them.* This is probably the most important similarity, because it gets to the heart of what addiction is all about. Sarah copes with the emptiness in her life by filling it with a strict schedule of activities. Clarice copes with the pain of her husband's rejection (and, yes, the "pain in her past") by anesthetizing herself with food, music, and comforting religious thoughts. Unfortunately, these activities are not really "fixing" anything in the long run.

Figure 2

A "QUICK FIX" SOCIETY

Let's face it—we are a society which wants a quick fix for everything. Whether it's fast food, a zip-lock for this, a little quickie for that, instant printing, or one-minute photo development, we want it *now*. Hence, many of us have gotten in the habit of trying to find quick fixes for any unpleasant feelings or experiences.

When we feel depressed, we pop a pill. When we feel uneasy, we eat. When we sense impending boredom coming our way, we head for the mall. Something inside us says, "Oh, no, here it comes . . . I'll split!" As a result of this mind-set, many of us become master escape artists, hiding behind substances or activities that seem to bring us momentary relief. Harmless . . . or is it?

Drug abuse is on the rise, alcoholism continues to erode our society, teen suicides are increasing. These deadly developments represent too permanent an answer for our temporary problems. And surely they are extreme examples that underscore the philosophy of millions of people: "I want a stress-free life, and I want it *now*!"

"Things are so bad with Joe and me, I spent the night with Mike."

"After I heard about Mom's surgery, I ate a whole bag of chocolate-chip cookies."

"God just doesn't seem to answer my prayers, so that's why I'm drinking again."

It's no wonder people fall into such unhealthy mental habits. A recent article in *New Woman* magazine[1] provides the following "Pick-Me-Ups; They're Fun, They're Fast, and They WORK!" Believe it or not, here are several women's thoroughly serious suggestions for escaping depression:

> BARBARA: "I head home for lunch and tune my TV to *All My Children*. My husband teases me about my addiction—my therapy—and I keep it a secret from most friends and co-workers. . . ."
> MARCIA: "I love sexy novels, and I'm always in the middle of at least three. I keep one on my night stand for bedtime reading; another in my glove compartment (to get me through the rush hour); and a third in my purse. . . ."
> KATHY: "I cure my depression by shopping. Nothing can compare with treating myself to a new outfit. . . ."
> RITA: "I find comfort in food. . . ."
> KAREN: "My pick-me-up is fantasized revenge. I write nasty letters to my clients but never mail them. . . ."

What surprised and bothered me about these suggestions was that they all recommended "fix" behavior as a cure for

---

1. Barbara Smalley, "10 Ways to Feel Better Fast," *New Woman,* August 1988, 47.

discomfort. Giving such advice to people seeking an "out" for depression is like advising a drug addict to work in a pharmacy!

Of course, not all escapes—not even some of the ones listed above—are unhealthy *in themselves*. We twentieth-century humans need a little diversion from our humdrum routine or from the stresses of daily life. A trip to the movies, a long walk, a favorite snack, a call to a friend, a good book, an evening at the theater—all can help us rest and restore our spirits.

But the trouble is, even these "harmless" or "healthy" diversions, under the right conditions, can become the object of private obsessions. That's why we need to ask ourselves this rather critical question about *any* activity:

```
                 Do I have it?

                      or

               Does it have me?
```

FIXES THAT DON'T FIX ANYTHING!

Here are some feelings and concerns that can lead us to seek a "fix" and make us prone to develop a hidden addiction:

fear	guilt
envy	anger
grief	jealousy
suspicion	desire
disappointment	low self-worth
boredom	loneliness

Not in any particular order, here are a few of the compulsive behaviors we may adopt to "fix" our negative feelings:

lying	working too much
overeating	cheating
overspending	compulsive gambling
inappropriate sexual behavior	gossip
complaining	TV watching

Ultimately, an addiction emerges from the repeated pattern of attempting to fix discomfort through compulsive behavior. (For more examples of "fixing" behaviors, see the list "Private Obsessions under Glass" on p. 49).

The trouble, of course, is that "fixes" are temporary. Although they may relieve negative feelings for awhile, their effects soon wear off, leaving us to "try again." The resulting pattern of discomfort, "fix," and recurring discomfort leads naturally into addictive behavior.

An added complication is that either the compulsive behavior itself or the resulting obsession with it brings *additional* discomfort in the form of guilt. We may feel guilty because we believe the actual behavior is wrong or because we know, deep down, that our "good" behavior has us hooked. Either way, our unresolved guilt eats at our sense of self-worth and fans feelings of inferiority. And the resulting discomfort starts the "fix" cycle all over again.

As an example, let's take a look at how a sexual addiction can develop. Certainly not everyone who has a fleeting lustful thought or sexual fantasy will become a sex addict. But this is what *can* happen:

- a feeling of emotional discomfort or pain,
- a sexual experience that temporarily "fixes" the sense of discomfort,
- a mental connection (not always conscious) of the activity with relief of discomfort,
- continued discomfort (because the "fix" is temporary),
- the thought of relieving that discomfort with sex,
- a failed attempt to control thoughts, resulting in an obsession with sex,
- a gradual increase in compulsive sexual activity,
- a repeated return of discomfort, this time accompanied by guilt and regret,
- cover-up and denial,
- repeated cycle of pain, obsessive sexual thoughts, compulsive sexual behavior, and denial,
- development of a habitual pattern of compulsive sexual behavior—an addiction.

ALL OR NOTHING

Here's another pattern. Those of us who have a tendency toward addictive behavior often find ourselves in a "feast or famine" situation. Instead of pursuing moderation, we swing from one extreme to another. A food addiction, for example, might be pictured as shown in figure 3:

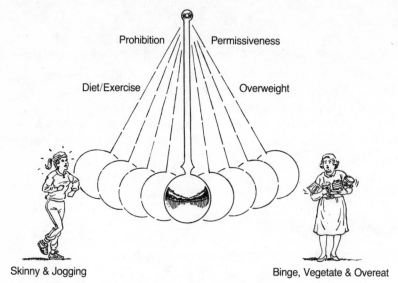

Figure 3 — The Pendulum

Many other process addictions seem to work the same way. The workaholic either clocks eighteen hours in an exhausting, overly scheduled day or sits inactive—a true couch potato. The romance addict either spends every waking moment analyzing a love affair or goes into a shell, refusing to be involved with anyone. The cleanliness freak's house either gleams, or it becomes a health hazard!

This "all or nothing" behavior leads me to wonder whether the quest for *perfection* is the root of our addictive behaviors. We want to have everything perfectly our way— or we don't want to play at all. Here are some ideas on the way our quest for perfection could be related to private obsessions:

PERFECTIONIST QUEST	PRIVATE OBSESSION
a perfect body	physical fitness nutrition or diet body building avoiding illness
perfect knowledge	education reading New Age and/or the occult
perfect self-knowledge	self-analysis pop-psych self-help books therapy
perfect performance of a job	work house cleaning parenting
human perfection	volunteerism church taking care of others
having all needs perfectly met	shopping success entertainment (TV, light reading, movies, etc.)
being loved perfectly	romance relationships sex
perfect happiness or enjoyment (never being bored)	entertainment thrills or adventure gambling

Whoever said we were supposed to be perfect or to experience perfection, anyway? We all know, consciously, that "nobody's perfect." And yet some deep urge within us, instilled in us from the beginning of time, makes us keep on trying to "get it right." And since nothing on earth is capable of granting that perfect satisfaction we seek, we are continually dissatisfied. We keep looking for perfect "fixes" in activities and relationships that are incapable of "fixing" us completely.

Perhaps that's why "cross addictions" are so common. We turn from one solution to another—for instance, from cigarettes to overeating to overinvolvement in self-help groups. And none of them provides the long-term comfort and freedom we yearn for. In fact, instead of "fixing" our pain, our obsessions, compulsions, and addictions just make matters worse.

FIXING YOUR "FIX" BEHAVIOR— A SPIRITUAL APPROACH

Our world is very influenced by psychology, a relatively young field that provides many theories and solutions for human behavior. Psychology, in fact, is often presented as the solution to our private obsessions. But while psychology can provide us with very helpful insights about the inner workings of our hearts and minds, it has built-in limitations when it comes to providing deep, long-term solutions to problems such as hidden obsessions. (Perhaps that's why so many people go through years of therapy without much improvement—sometimes, in the process, becoming addicted to therapy!) The reason for this, I believe, is that psychology as it is usually practiced ignores a vital aspect of our beings—our spirituality.

Spirituality has to do with our connection to a "Higher Power" and our response to the way that Higher Power has ordered the universe. As a Christian, I know that Higher Power as God, and I am convinced that true freedom grows from a relationship to God that is made possible by faith in Jesus Christ. In later chapters, I hope I can show some reasons why. But whatever your beliefs, an openness to a spiritual approach to healing can make a huge difference in overcoming private obsessions.

The point of seeking a spiritual solution to our problems is that those problems, in part, are spiritual in nature. They involve a deep-seated feeling of somehow being at odds with the universe, an inner hunger that no amount of "fix" behavior can satisfy and that psychology alone can't address.

If we were to contrast psychology's approach to obsessive behavior with that of spirituality, it might look something like this:

PSYCHOLOGY SAYS:	SPIRITUALITY SAYS:
The addicted person needs a personality change.	Yes, but the addicted person needs a change of heart, a spiritual awakening.
Analysis and mental catharsis must take place.	Yes, but this means a person must examine herself, confess her faults and become honest about her "moral inventory."
The obsessive individual withdraws from life, is abnormally self-oriented, and removes himself from society.	Yes, but this is because the obsessive person's problem is self-centeredness. Because of this self-absorption, the compulsive person forgets about her fellow human beings.
The obsessive person must make her way back into life. She should find a place of belonging in her career, social life, and hobbies to replace her obsessive needs.	Yes, but the obsessive person must also learn to love other people as she learns to love and serve God. She must "lose life to find it," discovering through her spiritual life the inner resources to meet her own need.

This book, in essence, follows the spirituality approach to healing. It assumes that understanding the problem through psychology is not enough, that people with private obsessions need the kind of deep change that comes only through facing themselves honestly and then relying on God's help.

I'm in good company with this approach. It is very similar to that of Alcoholics Anonymous, whose "Twelve-Step Program" has helped countless alcohol addicts over the years. AA's worldwide network of recovery "support groups" has expanded to include programs for those addicted to drugs, the families of addicts, and—significantly—those with process addictions such as compulsive overeating and gambling. No one can dispute their phenomenal success in dealing with the seriously addicted.

What many people don't realize, however, is that AA's Twelve Steps are biblically based. Originally called "Ten Decisions for Wholeness," they were developed at Oxford University at around the turn of the twentieth century, in the wake of the Wesleyan revival movement. And although they refrain from specifically "religious" language to avoid alienating those addicts who shy away from religion, the solution they offer is a spiritual one. (The Twelve Steps of Alcoholics Anonymous are listed on page 102.)

There is only one requirement for those who attend AA meetings: They must simply admit their "unmanageable" lifestyle and their need for divine help to overcome it. In these meetings, therefore, men and women are bonded together by their confessed weaknesses and not by their strengths. And then they are encouraged to turn to the only One who is capable of providing them with a lasting fix.

"Fine," you ask, "But what does all this have to do with Sarah's immaculately clean house? With Clarice's Jack Hayford tapes? Or with that 'friend' of mine who's just so compulsive?" Or with you or me?

I'm getting to that. But first, let's look at some of the most common forms of private obsessions. They are listed on the following pages under the heading, "Private Obsessions under Glass."

private obsessions under glass
a sampling of hidden addictions

The following is a lay person's descriptive list that describes, in practical terms, some of the crippling habits we term "private obsessions." The list is by no means exhaustive or complete, and it isn't full of medical or psychological terms. It is simply offered to illustrate the kinds of things of which we all need to beware. As you read it, keep in mind that many compulsive behaviors are considered socially acceptable— even socially admirable (for instance, volunteerism, workaholism, and so on)—but all meet our criteria of serving either to tranquilize or stimulate a person and "fix" an impending undesirable feeling.

Note also that the list contains only process addictions *and a few minor substance addictions that respond to the recovery process outlined in this book. This means that some of the most well-known addictions, such as alcoholism and drug addictions, have been omitted from the list.*

ADVENTURE SEEKER: Takes risks either in relationships or in physical activities. Thrives on challenges, conflicts, stimulation, and/or fantasy but has trouble getting motivated in "ordinary" situations.

ADVICE ADDICT: Hooked on horoscopes, "Dear Abby," radio call-in shows, and similar sources of advice. Continually communicates about personal problems and seeks out the opinions of "experts"—but seldom really acts on those opinions. Views self as inadequate in the decision-making process without outside input.

ANALYSIS ADDICT: Captivated by introspection and self-analysis. Continually seeks insight and personal self-knowledge. Craves therapy, counseling, and emotional support.

ANGER ADDICT: Controlled and frequently motivated by inner hostility and frustration. Energized by the adrenalin rush caused by angry outbursts and the sense of self-pride in having "taught them a lesson."

BARGAIN HUNTER: Obsessed with finding "deals." More interested in the bargain than in the object itself and so often ends up buying unneeded or even unwanted items.

BOOKWORM/BOOKAHOLIC: "Mainlines" books, articles, newspapers or other forms of the printed page—either fiction or nonfiction. May be obsessed with the need to seek knowledge or simply crave vicarious emotional stimulation. Tends to focus on one particular kind of book—romance novels, mysteries, self-help books—and may be cross-addicted to the specific subject of the book (for instance, World War II or cookbooks).

CAFFEINE JUNKIE: Hooked on coffee, tea, colas, or over-the-counter pep pills. Note: This is a minor substance addiction, but it responds quite well to the self-help techniques described in this book.

CARETAKER: Bases self-esteem on how much can be done for others. Needs dependent personalities to "do for." Closely related to Volunteer, and other "good girl" dependencies.

CHURCHAHOLIC/RELIGIOUS ADDICT: Addicted to the friendships and fellowship as expressed in a religious setting. Uses the pleasant feelings derived from church gatherings as a substitute for dealing with nitty-gritty realities and as a way to avoid responsibility. Churchaholics tend to have "toxic faith," which my friend Steve Arterburn describes as "a destructive and dangerous relationship with a religion that allows the religion, not the relationship with God, to control a person's life. Many seek a god drug that will wipe out consequences and quickly ease all hurts."[1]

---

1. Stephen Arterburn, *Toxic Faith* (Nashville: Thomas Nelson, 1990).

COMPUTER FETISH: May be obsessed with programming, games, electronic bulletin boards, or simply "putting together a system."

CONTROL ARTIST/POWERHOLIC: Must always be in charge of people and circumstances. Uses various forms of manipulative behavior to cause others to perform in desired manner and experiences severe frustration when power over others is hindered or removed.

COUPON CLIPPER: Habitually searches for money-saving coupon offers or refunds. Spends more time fixated on the coupon fetish than is ever justified by the money saved. Closely related to Bargain Hunter.

DEPRESSION JUNKIE: Gets perverse pleasure out of being continually miserable. Unconsciously or consciously enjoys the attention that continual misery and negativism brings. May be an Analysis Addict as well. (Note: Depression itself is *not* a hidden obsession. It is a normal reaction to grief and loss and may also involve chemical imbalance in the brain. But like any other activity, it can *become* a private obsession when it becomes a habitual way of thinking.)

EATING ADDICT: Preoccupied with food and dependent on some way of relating to food. This could include overindulging, bingeing/purging, compulsive dieting, or fasting. Preoccupation with certain foods—such as sugar— are possible. Private obsessions with food can lead to weight problems or to eating disorders such as anorexia nervosa and/or bulimia.

EDUCATION FREAK: "Career student," continually seeking knowledge but seldom applying acquired skills in a practical manner. May be fascinated with the learning process, the process of compiling information or doing research, or simply hooked on the heady give-and-take of academic life.

ENTERTAINMENT JUNKIE: Hooked on the distraction provided by television, movies, music, theater, amusement parks, video or parlor games, cards, and so on.

ENVIER/COVETER: Finds no contentment with present realities, continually absorbed by comparison of self with others. Obsessed with "keeping up with the Joneses." Forever craves situations and/or possessions of another; this craving fuels greed and avarice.

FITNESS FREAK: Insatiable need for physical exercise, conditioning, working out. Preoccupied with physical appearance, physical strength, diet, and exercise. Can lead to eating disorders, multiple cosmetic surgeries, or overspending on fitness paraphernalia.

GADGET JUNKIE: Cannot resist gadgets and gizmos—watches and clocks with bells and whistles, electronic schedulers, three-in-one tools—anything intriguing, electronic, or miniaturized.

GAMBLER: Hooked on the lure of lady luck. The "high" comes from the prospect of winning, whether at Las-Vegas-style casinos, Bingo tables, or the lottery counter. This obsession usually involves money but may include any risk-taking activity, including daredevil adventures, sports betting, or gaming pools. It is therefore closely related to Thrill Seeker.

GOSSIP: Finds pleasure and a sense of power through searching out hidden, unknown information about others and then "spreading the news." Gets stimulation from being "the first to know" and "first to tell." This obsession may lure the addict into spreading tales about others, indulging in character assassination, destroying reputations, and judgmentalism.

HEALTH NUT: Obsessed with staying healthy through nutrition, exercise, better understanding of how the body works, etc. This person may have a pharmacy in the medicine cabinet, a medical library on the bookshelves, and a health-food store in the kitchen. Hypochondriacs are variations on this theme.

HOMOSEXUALITY HOOKEE: Has a sex or romance addiction which focuses on persons of the same sex. Can include abnormal curiosity, voyeurism, or preoccupation with perversions or sexual abnormalities.

HOUSECLEANING HOOKEE: Need for order demands
continuous commitment to clinical cleanliness. Addict will
often avoid relationships while controlling physical environ-
ment. "Too-Tidy-Heidi" requires immaculate surroundings
which limit activities and curb social life.

HYPOCHONDRIAC: A form of Health Nut. Worries continually about state of his or her health and imagines every
perceived symptom is a sign of disease.

MUSIC FREAK: Requires continuous melodic sounds at all
times whether in car, home or workplace. Music is used to
drown out relationship realities or to feed fantasies such as
on-stage performance or romance.

NICOTINE FREAK: Unable to stop smoking because of
withdrawal symptoms both physical *and emotional* in nature.
The 1989 Surgeon General's Report stated "Smoking is as
much an addiction as cocaine usage."

OCCULT ADDICT: Entranced by mysterious powers and
knowledge of "the hidden and unknown." These are sought
through witchcraft, card and palm reading, seances, New Age
practices. This dangerous seeking after power and knowledge
of the past or future can lead a person into dark realms of
Satanic activity.

PACK RAT: Derives a false sense of security by holding on
to material possessions—unable to part with anything. This
form of private obsession includes the hoarder, the chronic
saver, the compulsive "collector," of files, photo albums,
memorabilia and "great bargains." May or may not be a
Shopaholic as well.

PEOPLE PLEASER: Unable to say "no" to anyone. Habitually denies own desires and values to seek peace at all costs.
This form of private obsession related to Caretaker and often
provides a target for Control Artist.

PERFECTIONIST: Depressed by the flaws and blemishes of
self and others and requires unrealistic personal flawlessness.
Cannot rest when things are not in order. Leaves many tasks

uncompleted; procrastinates because of inability to do things "right."

PET FREAK: Obsessed with caretaking of animals and the affection they provide. Often alters lifestyle dramatically to accommodate beloved pets.

READING ADDICT: "Mainlines" books with an incessant desire for escape through fantasy and living life through the printed page. Tends to focus on one particular kind of book— romance novels, mysteries, self-help books—and may be cross-addicted to the specific subject of the book (for instance, romance or knowledge). See Bookworm.

RELATIONSHIP ADDICT: Believes he or she is only validated by being involved in successful relationships, especially with the opposite sex. May be closely related to romance addiction or compulsive caretaking.

ROMANCE ADDICT: Vicariously lives out romantic fantasies through the lives of others (real or imaginary) or is hooked on the "high" of alluring tales of romance. Common cross-addictions: Soap Opera Addict, Bookworm..

SEX ADDICT: Intoxicated by any medium (printed page, screen, fantasy, or real-life activities) where nudity and sexual fantasies are acted out. Insatiable craving for sexual gratification.

SHOPAHOLIC: Fixated on the process of shopping and the ensuing collecting of goods—necessary or unnecessary. This condition supersedes a commitment to financial obligations and can lead to running up large debts. Many, but not all, shopaholics are also Bargain Hunters.

SLEEP SEEKER: Escapes reality and pressures by sleeping late into the day, napping, or oversleeping, in the process developing chronic fatigue. Common cross-addiction of Depression Junkies.

SOAP OPERA ADDICT: Hooked on the ongoing tales of imaginary characters portrayed on day and/or nighttime soaps. Arranges daily routine for viewing and obsessively catches up on missed episodes. Fictional characters become real people in the mind—acquaintances and friends. Often cross-addicted with Romance Addiction.

SOCIAL JUNKIE: Chatty Cathy has a compulsion to be seen and heard in social settings. Continually seeks approval and recognition through social interaction and personal appearance. Craves affirmation through personal interaction.

SPORTS FANATIC: Addicted to physical participation in sports activities or to vicarious enjoyment via observation and knowledge of sporting events, sports stars, statistics, or records. This private obsession includes both the "super fan" and/or "super jock."

SUCCESSAHOLIC: Motivated by perfectionism, fear, competitiveness, and pride to "get ahead." Winning is paramount, and achieving and accomplishing goals are compulsory for this upwardly mobile type, whose compulsion can make him/her become ruthless and even unethical.

SUPERPARENT (often SUPERMOM): Fixates on the intricate details of children's lives—is anxious, doting, and overprotective. Often driven by desire to live life through children or to distract oneself from a flawed marriage. This kind of overattentive parenting produces smothering rather than mothering, bothering rather than fathering.

TELEPHONE JUNKIE: "Romancing the Phone" leads to secret conversations at all hours, gathering information, or sharing intimacies (resulting in mind-altering phone bills). Individual may be unable to leave house because of fear of missing calls and often relates best to the outside world without face-to-face contact, confrontation, or personal responsibility.

VICTIM (OR MARTYR): Swallowed up in self-pity due to life's mishaps or some single traumatic event. This addict feels slighted and taken advantage of repeatedly, and expects the worst.

VOLUNTEER: Tends to offer help compulsively and often without counting the cost to current commitments and priorities.

The "I'll do it . . ." syndrome may develop from a desire for social involvement, a gratified sense of responsibility (without having to qualify), or a need to be needed. This sometimes amounts to a "legal" escape from such required duties as parenting, housekeeping, or building deep personal relationships. See Compulsive Caretaker.

WORKAHOLIC: Obsesses with job-related activity (including housework), often putting in eighteen-plus hours a day. Frantic commitment to responsibilities and duties serves as an anesthetic to deaden the effects of intimate pain and fear. May use travel and phones or other ways of removing self from conscious involvement with an unsatisfactory personal life.

WORRYWART: Habitually focuses on problems, small and/ or large, and gets a perverse pleasure in playing the martyr. The sense of anxiety provides distraction from more significant problems, and solution of circumstances does not remove the worry.

3

hooked on a feeling

confronting your relationship addictions

"Lee, I've got to talk to you about my husband."

"Excuse me, Mrs. Ezell. I'd like to ask you a question about something. See, there's this man. . . ."

"Oh, Lee, I'm so in love, and I'm so miserable! What can I do?"

In the past few years, I have spoken all over America at women's conferences, churches, and conventions. I've talked to hundreds and hundreds of women. And in all my listening, I have discovered there is one form of private obsession that is so common, even among mature women, that I think it deserves a chapter of its own. I'm talking about relationship addiction.

RELATIONSHIP ADDICTS

"Man Junkies," I call them—women who are strung out on their need for romance and the yearning to be "with" somebody—no matter what. Many would-be good relationships are sabotaged by this kind of private obsession. Being "hooked on a man" has the power both to destroy good marriages and to hold destructive marriages together. Although no chemical substance is involved, man junkies are just as dependent on

substance is involved, man junkies are just as dependent on
their relationships as heroin addicts are addicted to their drug.

Although the greatest relationship-addiction problems
involve male-female liaisons, this form of private obsession is
not limited to mixed doubles. An unhealthy relationship can
develop between best friends, who become possessive, jeal-
ous, and exclusive to the alienation of the families involved.
A parent may become obsessed with her child, smothering
instead of mothering. And addictive relationships can also
develop between a spiritual leader and a follower, a boss and
an employee—in almost any kind of association, close or
distant. Often one who becomes "hooked on a person" dis-
plays a pattern of a lifetime of unhealthy relationships with
both family and friends.

Robin Norwood reinforces this point in her book, *Women
Who Love Too Much.*

> We use relationships in the same way that we use
> our addictive substance to take our pain away. . . .
> As long as we are bent on escaping ourselves and
> avoiding our pain we stay sick. The harder we try
> and the more avenues of escape we pursue the
> sicker we get as we compound addictions with
> obsessions.[1]

NOT REALLY LOVE

When we use the term "private obsession," we recall that
we are talking about "something" we feel we *must* have. And
for a great many people—especially women—that "something" we think we need is another person.

When we don't receive the affection or attention we think
we need, therefore, we become upset. Then we try too hard,
almost like puppy dogs who will do anything—wag our tails,
fetch a stick, jump through a hoop—just for a pat on the head.

---

1. Robin Norwood, *Women Who Love Too Much,* (Los Angeles: St.
Martin's, 1985), 137.

Or we withdraw, hurt, and pull back from any emotional involvement. Or we get angry and lash out. What did we do to deserve this? Is this how our love is rewarded?

But *is* it love? When viewed from this perspective, a relationship addiction is actually an emotion-backed demand. It is a way of using the other person to supply something we feel we need. Our attachment arises out of our own incompleteness rather than concern for the other person. We mistake it for love, but it's just the opposite.

That's why it's important to ask ourselves, in any important attachment or relationship:

Am I in love with

a person

or

a feeling?

The struggles of the single mom make her especially susceptible to becoming dependent on relationships. In the process of reeling from the tragedy of divorce or widowhood and struggling with the need to reconfirm her sexuality (not to mention meet financial challenges), the single mom often convinces herself a new "daddy" is the answer for herself and her family.

Eventually she may meet a man who promises that "all her problems will be solved" by marrying him. What perfect timing! She feels "peace" and "relief" with him. She wants to be married again. And so she's ready to tie the knot.

Unfortunately, marriage is far too permanent an answer for this lady's temporary problems. Does she know enough or care enough about the man himself? Is his agenda the same as hers? Is she looking for a partner or a rescuer? Many a single mom, in my experience, is hooked on a feeling . . . the fantasy that a relationship is all she needs to solve her dilemma. If she makes her decision only on the basis of her need, she may be setting herself up for nothing but heartbreak.

THE ENABLEMENT SCENARIO

When we base our relationship choices on our own needs
and deficiencies, we set ourselves up for unhealthy—even
abusive—relationships. Because we are convinced that any
kind of relationship is better than none at all, we may become
unwitting participants in our own pain.

A friend of mine—Marcie, we will call her—was a true
"man junkie." She was so hooked on her husband that her
clinging was stifling their marriage. To complicate matters,
her husband wanted a woman (any woman) who was less
attached, less like a parasite. Before long, he found himself
one in another town. Time and again he would leave his wife
to live with that woman. Marcie would remain silent, except
for times when she covered up for him. She didn't dare
confront him—she was too afraid he would leave her.

Of course Marcie's root problem lay in the way she viewed
herself. She felt she could not be whole without her husband.
As a result, she became the chief "enabler" of his abusive
behavior. She was willing to suffer any abuse he dished out
just to "hold the marriage together."

Obviously, Marcie's husband was in the wrong—but her
behavior was sick as well. Her whole relationship to him was
based on martyrdom. In her desperate need for a relationship,
she had set herself up for rejection and distance. And their
marital coldness and separation only confirmed the fact that
her husband doubted her worth.

RELATIONSHIP ADDICTION AND ABUSE

A lot has been written about why women stay in abusive
situations. There are many factors—fear, lack of economic
options, irrational guilt ("If I were a better wife, he wouldn't
act like this").

But I can't help but believe that relationship addiction keeps
a lot of women in destructive relationships. They stay because
their relationships—bad as they are—fill their addictive need.

I also believe that a misunderstanding of the biblical principle of wifely "submission" has been a culprit in some abusive

marriages. The way some Christians understand it, submission really means "submersion" or "suppression." But the Bible never speaks of biblical "subjection" with the implication that a woman should subject herself to abusive behavior. I believe our misinterpretation of this biblical principle has fanned the fires of much angry feminism. And we in the church must swallow hard and bear the responsibility for the violations that misrepresentations of this principle have fostered.

Jesus Christ presented himself to us as the great liberator of women. He related to them as responsible people; he gave them dignity. Yet, as I was growing up, my own mother was so convinced that to end her marriage to my father would make her a "failure" that she endured (along with all of us children) a battering and abusive husband.

"MY OTHER HALF"

Any time we women believe we are not whole without a man, we are ready for a fall. It is this kind of faulty thinking that causes a woman to marry someone who provides something she lacks—her "other half." And that, again, is basing a relationship on need, not on love—on a feeling rather than a person.

Perhaps one woman feels she needs to be more adventuresome. And so she marries a real risk taker—who risks her life's savings as well as his neck. A practical-minded woman may seek out a "romantic" (who just happens to romance others besides her!). A quiet woman may marry "the life of the party"; a weak woman may seek a caretaker.

If we feel we are lacking some aspect of our personality, the answer is not to become involved with someone who provides that "missing" part of us. A much healthier strategy is either to develop that quality in ourselves or to decide it is not important. Whatever we do, we must resist fooling ourselves into thinking that "the right man" (or friend, or boss, or pastor) could fill in that "gap" in ourselves.

A faulty sense of self-worth—a sense of being incomplete or inadequate—is the foundation for relationship addiction. A relationship addict floods her mind with thoughts of another person in an effort to fill the holes in her self-esteem. The lower a woman's self-esteem, the more she will be apt to believe that someone else holds the key to her happiness. And the more susceptible she will be to developing a relationship addiction.

A woman needs to be healed and whole on the inside before she is able to choose whether or not she wishes another "attachment." When she is made whole, she is better equipped either to stay single or to marry. In either case, she will feel like an autonomous whole person, not a partial person "hooked" on the fruitless task of completing herself through another person.

A SENSE OF IDENTITY

We can be sure of one thing. The stronger our sense of our own unique value and worth, the less subject we will be to being controlled by a private obsession. And this is particularly true in the case of relationship junkies. It is so unfair and untruthful of us to attach ourselves to another person—be it a spouse, a child, a friend, or even a minister—and to expect them to rectify whatever our lives lack.

No human being has the power to validate us or complete us. That is an inside job, truly the work of the Spirit of God alone. It only comes when the Spirit convinces us from within that we have value and worth. The experiences of deep friendship or "being in love" and the institution of marriage are not supposed to make us into what we hope to become.

Tony Campolo, a provocative and entertaining speaker, tells of a husband who was about to leave his wife and three children. The husband told Tony, "I feel cramped. Marriage doesn't allow me to be all that I can be."

Tony wisely responded, alluding to a popular recruitment slogan for the military, "Do you want to be all that you can be? Then join the army!"

Tony is right. The purpose of relationships is not to make us whole people.

Now, don't make the mistake of thinking that I'm giving you "permission" to end any important relationship in your life—especially marriage!—as soon as it stops "feeling good." The purpose of relationships isn't just to make us feel good, either.

But too many women are reaching out for the women's magazines which promise them nothing but rainbows in their relationships. The cover story is headlined, "Making Him Love You Again." We grab it, read every word, and try to follow its advice. We want to help our man become what we want and "need" him to be. Not only is this an impossibility. It's a treacherous, tender trap. It leads us to be relationship junkies instead of whole, healthy people involved in relationships.

HEALTHY RELATIONSHIPS

Most people believe that love "feels good." The reasons this is true are very psychologically complicated—which is probably why relationship addictions develop. But comparing some of the characteristics of healthy and unhealthy relationships can help us diagnose our possible relationship addiction.

UNHEALTHY RELATIONSHIPS	HEALTHY RELATIONSHIPS
You fear letting go.	You enjoy life with or apart from the other.
You are consumed with the other person.	You feel the freedom to ask for what you need.
You fear any risk or change.	Each of you promotes the personal growth of the other.
You feel your life is expressed through another.	You have stopped trying to control the other person.
You believe your love can change the other person.	You appreciate the self-containment and self-sufficiency of the other.

You feel "abandoned" when separated.	Each of you is able to say, "I am enough by myself alone."
You feel incomplete without the other person.	Self-esteem is growing through your relationship.
You attend to the other person's needs while neglecting and disregarding your own needs.	You are developing the habit of not denying your own needs; you are learning to express your opinions and feelings freely.

Reading these characteristics, you may notice something about the description of unhealthy relationships: they make up what could be interpreted as a "bond of love." Being in "bondage" or in some way enslaved or tied to another person is not a healthy attitude. In fact, such an attachment creates strain that could stifle any relationship. Healthy love provides freedom, not bondage.

"Man junkies" often have the feeling that they cannot live without a man. Once they have him, however, they feel they can't live with him. One of my four sisters, who was between marriages, confessed to me, "It's hell to be married, and it's hell not to be married. We're all in the same boat."

Well, I say, "Get out of the boat!" If you are in that kind of a negative position with regards to relationships, you are sinking. Get out! Grab something that is floating. Then, like a good surfer, catch a wave.

I am not suggesting that being in a relationship with another human being (who happens to be the opposite sex!) has to be a negative experience. Nor do I mean to suggest that living alone is the best possible way to live. Let's face it, gals: we women are not the easiest people to live with either. But choosing to be married does not mean resigning ourselves to be married.

Getting free from our addictive-relationship behavior frees us from fear and enables us to communicate our frustrations, our sorrows, and our joys. Perhaps for the first time we'll actually enjoy a healthy relationship.

THE UNDEPENDENT WOMAN

My husband, Hal, and I are beginning to share the kind of life that is rich in collaboration and mutual enjoyment on many levels. We are both autonomous individuals with our own careers who have made the healthy choice to be committed to marriage. I think we have come to many of our conclusions because of the extent to which each of us travels and the many separations that we therefore must experience.

I no longer practice what one woman termed "window sitting"—where I longingly wait for him to come home in order to resume life. This is not to say we don't enjoy our times together. On the contrary, our separations make us cherish our shared times even more.

Much of this autonomy, in practical terms, has to do with our "stages" in life, of course. Hal and I have our intensive child-rearing years behind us and have a little more freedom to come and go. If you are a mother of younger children, on the other hand, you may find yourself waiting a lot—waiting for soccer practice to be over, waiting for everyone to get home for supper, and so on. But even in those circumstances, the question becomes: what are we doing with our "waiting" time? Are we waiting for our kids to grow up? Or are we growing too?

BREAKING THE ADDICTION

How about it? Do you think you may be a "man junkie" or another kind of relationship addict? Before we go on, why don't you take a few minutes to complete Self-Test #2, "Are You Ruled by Your Relationships?" You may find it most enlightening.

Even if you find you aren't "relationship healthy," not to worry! A healthy love relationship is possible when we can reach out to another person from our strength and not from our weakness. This is why we must repair our own spirits and not look to another human being to do that for us.

First of all, if you've determined that you are, in fact, hooked on relationships, don't be surprised if you have to suffer through some emotional withdrawal symptoms. As you try to break the habit of turning to relationships for an emotional fix, there will be times when you feel abandoned and lonely.

The steps outlined in the second part of this book will help you work through this pain. But it will also help to remember that *no* relationship is capable of yielding us true satisfaction. If we are to be whole, healthy people, our sources of satisfaction must come from within. When we decide to be free of love addiction, we agree to release our desire to be controlled or to control another person.

As we attempt to yield to the Spirit of God within us, we must endeavor to become "inner directed" and not "other directed." Inner-directed people have an internal guidance system and don't need to rely solely on outside cues to decide what to do. Best of all, they aren't afraid to be alone! One of the joys of breaking relationship addictions is learning to enjoy and value our own company.

THE BOTTOM LINE

As we endeavor to free ourselves from our "attachment" to other people, it won't take us long to realize that we do need an attachment to *something*. In relationship addictions, as in all private obsessions, we remain unhappy because we are looking to the wrong source for satisfaction. We think we "hunger" for love, but human relationships were never meant to completely satisfy the gnawing emptiness inside of us.

Jesus told us, "Blessed are those who hunger and thirst after righteousness, for they shall be filled." Our hunger, therefore, needs to be a desire for satisfaction and contentment from within and not from without—not even from another person.

It is normal to desire companionship, closeness, and warmth. Without these characteristics we wouldn't be human. And there's no need to adopt an abrasive, touch-me-not attitude just to avoid unhealthy relationships. But we do need to focus our hopes on a more reliable, dependable source of comfort beyond spouses/lovers/partners. I am learning to abandon my fairy-tale thinking, as I rely on Christ, the "Prince of Peace" who, the Bible records, has faithfully promised never to leave me nor forsake me.

TO STAY OR NOT TO STAY

What about breaking up? Is it necessary to end a relationship in order to recover from a relationship addiction?

Simply put, the answer is no—although sometimes it helps.

In a marriage relationship, apart from abusive circumstances, I am convinced that ending it all is not the answer. We know the majority of people who divorce remarry. And of those who remarry, many again divorce. Calling it quits without having the satisfaction of knowing we've done everything we can to make it work out will only leave us with more regrets. If you are wrestling with a relationship addiction, you must grapple with an interior, not an exterior enemy. Patterns of wrongly relating can be corrected within the framework of marriage. Little by little, you can rid yourself of unhealthy patterns through the process outlined in the second half of the book.

If you are unmarried and not currently in a relationship, you can certainly work on your addiction patterns just as you are! In fact, you are probably in the best position of all to work through your "need" for a man.

If you are unmarried but in an unhealthy relationship, *perhaps* breaking it off will be the best answer for you. Believe me, it is *not* better to be in an unhealthy relationship than to have no relationship at all! But it's important to realize that the relationship addiction is essentially *your* problem. Just getting out of the relationship will not necessarily free you from being a relationship junkie!

Here are some ideas to help you decide whether breaking up is the appropriate thing to do. They are adapted in part from Dr. Howard Halpern's excellent book, *How to Break Your Addiction to a Person*[2]:

- *Attempt to separate yourself from that other person psychologically and, if possible, physically.* This will help you gain perspective for making your decision.
- *Ask yourself, like singer Peggy Lee, "Is that all there is?"* What is the point of this relationship? Is it positive, healthy, meant to be?

---

2. Howard M. Halpern, *How to Break Your Addiction to a Person* (New York: Bantam, 1983), 188–201.

- *Count the cost of breaking up.* It's important to foresee that the breaking up of a relationship will not be without pain. In some instances, it may also be necessary to consider the affect of a breakup on children, other family members, your finances, and so forth. The more deeply involved you are, the harder the breakup will be.
- *Check your belief system and work to develop a healthier outlook on relationships.* Ask yourself: What is the most important thing in life? What is the purpose of relationships? Does a relationship have to last forever in order to be meaningful? What can I put up with without endangering my integrity or my beliefs? Which is better—to end a relationship or to live with ongoing hatred, anger, fear, and dependence?
- *Confront your attachment hunger.* Ask: "Does my yearning and longing to be in this relationship (or any relationship) overshadow my true feelings?" Also ask yourself whether your desire to be with the other person comes from choice, or whether it's a matter of *need.* Identify and confront your attachment hunger to overrule its power to frighten and paralyze you.

BREAKIN' UP IS HARD TO DO

If you do decide that ending a relationship is a necessary part of ending your relationship addiction, be prepared for some pain. A popular, old song says, "Breakin' up is hard to do," and so it is! Bad investments cannot be written off without some loss, and the investments made in friendship or love are just as painful to lose as investments of money.

The fact that breakups are painful doesn't mean that the pain has to continue endlessly, however. Time truly does heal wounds. Sometimes, however, time pressure and responsibilities keep us from taking the time we need to mourn a lost relationship. As a result, our pain may be extended unnecessarily.

For this reason, I suggest that you schedule for yourself a time frame—a day, a weekend, or even a little longer—in which to specifically grieve and mourn for the loss of that relationship. Some pain may continue after that period has elapsed, but that period of specific mourning can give you a chance to deal constructively with the breakup and begin the healing process.

Make an effort to be totally alone for your mourning period. This may take some arranging on your part, but it will be worth it. During this time, you may want to talk out loud, weep, or express yourself in some other ways. Having a "witness" may keep you from being totally honest with yourself during this time.

Even though you are alone, however, remember that God is listening and that he understands your need for love even more than you do. Even in your aloneness, picture his reaching out his hand to say, "I love you."

Here are some suggested things to do during that mourning period:

(1) *Face the pain.* Feel it and do not try to avoid it or find a way around it. In particular, resolve not to numb the pain with other addictive behavior (such as Valium™, hot-fudge sundaes, or too much sleep).

(2) *Remember and relive the relationship.* Remember to recall the bad times as well as the good. Let yourself cry as much as you need to. But remember that this is your day to put to rest both the good and the bad of that relationship.

(3) *Review your memories.* Look at pictures, read letters, recall songs—whatever reminds you of the relationship.

(4) *Get angry—and get it over with.* This is your time not to let anger be buried alive in you anymore. You may want to speak out loud in the quiet of the room. The Bible says to "be angry and sin not." That means that anger is not a sin in itself. Anger is a natural emotion which is shared by the whole human community. But "buried" anger can "explode" at unforeseen times and can also affect your health, making you more prone to strokes, heart attacks, depression, and other problems. Take this time, therefore, to feel the intensity of your angry emotions and get them out of you. But note that your expression of anger should not be destructive to yourself or to your surroundings (save the glasses!).

(5) *Write a good-bye letter.* This is your "Dear John" note, intended to be your last communiqué. Whether or not you mail it is not really that important. The thought you put into

composing it is what matters. Writing it will help you think through and clarify your reasons for ending the relationship.

(6) *Take this chapter with you* to review and reinforce your analysis of why your relationship shouldn't continue. You may need some reinforcement!

(7) *Forgive and be forgiven.* Confess to God the failures that you recognize in yourself in that relationship and the toll that your addictive behavior may have taken on that relationship. And this is your time to ask your Heavenly Father to forgive you.

Do you need to forgive God? Many people discover that subconsciously they have held God responsible for the failure, for not making things work out right for them. Consciously forgive God—and yourself as well. And forgive the other person. Speak out loud, as an act of your will, that you forgive him or her for the hurt, the pain, the failure, the inability to behave in a more constructive way. (You may not *feel* forgiving. But the act of conscious forgiveness will be healing nevertheless.)

(8) *Consciously let go.* In your letting-go process, you may want to pray to finalize things. Here is a sample of what you might pray (adjust wording according to your understanding):

> Dear Father God,
>   Today I offer you my pain and grief over the loss of _____. I am attempting to let go and reach out for your healing. I ask you to take away the pain of the loss and replace it with your love and satisfaction. As I let go of _____ , I give him (her) over to you. And even though _____ is no longer in my life, I know I am not alone. I walk away from this time with you holding my hand. Thank you for receiving me, because of the sacrifice of Jesus Christ.

(8) *Be sure to have plenty of Kleenex!®*

When your special time of mourning is over, try to get out. Have dinner with a supportive friend and take time to share the experiences of your time alone. Express the effects your "time of mourning" has produced.

Then celebrate! You have begun to put the past behind you, and you are on the road to healing your relationship addiction.

self-test #2
are you ruled by your relationships?

As you answer the following questions, keep in mind all the different kinds of relationships you are involved in—husband/wife, male/female, parent/child, friends, neighbors, co-workers, and so on.

1. I find myself trying to take care of and nurture other adults. ___ True ___ False

2. I will do almost anything to keep a relationship from ending. ___ True ___ False

3. I usually wind up taking most of the responsibility in a relationship. ___ True ___ False

4. I accept the blame and feel guilty for most wrongs in a relationship. ___ True ___ False

5. Deep down inside, I do not believe I deserve to be loved like I want to be. ___ True ___ False

6. I say I'm just "being helpful," but I am usually trying to control a relationship. ___ True ___ False

7. I focus more on how I want a relationship to be than how it actually is. ___ True ___ False

8. I am addicted to the emotional pain caused by an unhealthy relationship. ___ True ___ False

9. I avoid dealing with my own problems by getting involved in other people's problems. ___ True ___ False

10. When I tell someone, "I love you," it really means "I need you." ___ True ___ False

11. I feel consumed in my relationships. ___ True ___ False

12. I have trouble defining where a person in my life ends and I begin. ___ True ___ False

13. I am afraid of risk, change, or the unknown in a relationship. ___ True ___ False

14. I experience a lot of things in my relationships, but true intimacy is not one of them. ___ True ___ False

15. There is a lot of psychological game playing in my relationship. ___ True ___ False

16. The only reason I "give" in a relationship is in hopes of getting something back. ___ True ___ False

17. Although I try to accept the people in my relationships, I can't help but feel we would all be better off if they would change. ___ True ___ False

18. When there is a problem to be solved in a relationship, I usually don't look to myself for the answer. ___ True ___ False

19. I expect to be loved unconditionally in a relationship. ___ True ___ False

20. I am hesitant to make any long-term commitment in a relationship. ___ True ___ False

21. I look to other people when I need to be affirmed and feel valuable. ___ True ___ False

22. I constantly bring up and dwell on the negative in a relationship. ___ True ___ False

23. I desperately desire to be close to someone, but I am too afraid. ___ True ___ False

24. I often find myself involved in a power struggle in my relationships. ___ True ___ False

25. I ask myself daily, "Why am I staying in this relationship?" ___ True ___ False

26. I think my hopes for a relationship are unrealistic, but I can't give them up. ___ True ___ False

27. I'm afraid that, if my current relationship ended, I would never find anyone else. ___ True ___ False

28. I think of breaking off the relationship, but I don't think I could ever get over the person. ___ True ___ False

29. I don't think I could ever bear being alone. ___ True ___ False

30. I honestly believe love is enough to make me happy. ___ True ___ False

31. I feel I need this person, but I'm not sure I actually love this person. ___ True ___ False

32. I believe if I work hard enough at it, the relationship will work out. ___ True ___ False

33. I stay in a relationship even when the negatives far outweigh the positives. ___ True ___ False

34. The more I think about ending a relationship, the harder I cling to it. ___ True ___ False

35. Whenever I make a move to end a relationship, I suffer severe withdrawal symptoms (loneliness, missing the person, etc.) and reestablish contact. ___ True ___ False

36. I didn't really choose this relationship . . . I just felt it was my only chance. ___ True ___ False

37. I think I am better off having a difficult relationship than none at all. ___ True ___ False

38. I usually attempt to meet the needs of the other person before I consider my own needs. ___ True ___ False

39. Without this person in my life, I would not feel complete. ___ True ___ False

40. I believe it's worth staying in a relationship no matter what the cost. ___ True ___ False

Having answered the above questions as honestly as possible, you probably have an idea whether you are ruled by your relationships and, if so, which relationship(s) rules you:

- *A score of 4 or fewer "Trues" indicates you are probably not ruled by your relationships* at the present time.
- *A score of 5-11 indicates you may be partly ruled by your relationships.*
- *A score of 13 or more indicates you may have a problem with relationship addiction.*

If your scoring on this or the other self-tests seems unclear or incomplete, why not have a close friend evaluate your answers? His or her caring opinion may shine a different light on your behavior and help you understand your actions.

4

---

a trio of
traps

work, shopping, and analysis addictions

For the past several years, I've been traveling. Lecturing all over America and in many places overseas. Talking—and listening—to women from all walks of life. In the process, I've discovered several private obsessions that seem particularly widespread among women. Easily the most prevalent is relationship addiction, which we discussed in the last chapter. But running close behind that are three other "crippling crutches":

- workaholism,
- compulsive shopping,
- analysis addiction.

Now wait! Don't turn to the next chapter without giving yourself a chance. Even if you don't identify with any of these private obsessions at first, you may find a little of yourself hidden in the pages to come. Read on!

WORKAHOLISM: GETTING THE JOB DONE—AND MORE

First of all, what is a workaholic—really? It's not necessarily a gray-suited executive burning midnight oil (although it could be). It could also be the homemaker who stays up late baking cookies and then has to mop the floor. It could be the teacher who spends vacations dreaming up extra-credit assignments. It could be the writer who never leaves the computer.

Basically, a workaholic is someone who is *always* minding his or her own business—no matter what the business is. How much work is enough? The workaholic invariably thinks: "Just a little more. . . ." This "aholism" is one of the most acceptable—even admired—addictions of our time, because our Western society places such a high value on productivity.

Workaholism is a particularly "popular" addiction right now. In the sixties, "laid back" was *in*. Today, "laid back" is another way of saying, "She's lazy and good-for-nothing." Compulsive work has become chic in America. You may even hear someone jokingly say, "Oh, I'm so compulsive," and find those words have a positive ring. "There's a person who gets things done," we think, silently applauding an industrious attitude.

If we are busy, we seem important. More significantly, we *feel* important—productive, worthwhile. But, although there is no value or premium to be found in laziness, the "hard work ethic" must be tempered with rest, reflection, and relaxation if we are to be healthy human beings.

Many workaholics (and I must include myself) have yet to understand that "self-worth" and "net worth" are not synonymous. Others (I include myself here, too) tend to equate self-worth with helping others or "making a contribution." Do you believe that you can be successful without an exhaustive list of accomplishments?

Today's women are especially vulnerable to falling into this trap because society expects so much of us. Women have taken on all sorts of activities outside the home—including full-time jobs. And yet, we are still supposed to be paragons of homemaking skill. We are to have a socially acceptable answer to, "Do you work? Well, what is it that you *do*?" We're supposed to be able to "bring home the bacon *and* fry it up in the pan." Meanwhile, we are to be glamorous, sensuous women and nurturing mothers as well! And too many women are trying to accomplish all that is expected. "Supermom" is a workaholic!

THE PROFESSION OBSESSION

Like our friend Sarah, who spent much of her energy simply being busy, the workaholic person tends to be admired as a "hard worker"—a "get things done" person. "She can do three things at once!" someone bragged to me about her friend. My question is, are we *supposed* to do three things at once?

I've already confessed to having a workaholic tendency, but I'm married to a man who at one time could have written the book on workaholism! My husband, Hal, worked for many years in the exciting field of law enforcement. His overtaxed schedule was full of high-intensity drug busts, stakeouts, investigations, and press conferences. Although he made attempts to control his hectic schedule, for many years it controlled him.

And he liked it! That's important to realize about workaholics. Most of them work too hard not because they have to (although that's the common excuse), but because work gives them pleasure or relief.

My husband began coming to grips with his workaholism when he realized that he was hooked on the "shot of adrenalin" that came from undercover operations and the media hounds who followed him. He also derived satisfaction from the fact that his work was beneficial to the public. Basically, his work made him feel good. And the habit of overindulging in something that "fixes" our bad feelings by making us feel good is a basic quality of addiction!

My work of writing and speaking makes me feel good, too. It's exciting to travel around the country. I enjoy knowing that I help people. Speaking in front of people can be an intoxicating "high." And so it was easy for me to become hooked on my work as well.

Both my husband and I come from the strong work-ethic era of "for God's sake, do something! Make something of your life. When in doubt—produce!" All this helped fuel our workaholic tendencies. Working hard—even too hard—made us feel worthwhile.

THE PRICE OF OVERWORK

Unfortunately, workaholism also took its toll on us. This became apparent to me when I went through one of my "health" reforms. One day it dawned on me that I was self-prescribing megavitamins for myself with names like "Zoom" and "Instant Energy." In the name of useful work, I was pushing my body beyond its normal capability. And I was becoming mentally and spiritually depleted as well.

And so, even though my husband's work and my own traveling and speaking were both rewarding and beneficial to others, we both reached a point where we had to ask ourselves whether God was imposing our impossible schedules upon us. When we honestly examined the facts, it was easy to see that he wasn't the one who had led us into such a feverish, panting frenzy, all in the name of public service. We were doing it to ourselves, and in the process we were wearing ourselves out.

The compulsive need to "do" has no mercy, and it presses a person beyond his normal endurance. Like engines constantly "revving" on high, workaholics wear themselves down. But they aren't the only ones who suffer. Many workaholics end up deserting their families emotionally. The body shows up for dinner; the brain stays at work. Or the body is present for the children, but the mind is still "on the job."

Workaholism is not always based on the urge to be productive. Sometimes it is rooted simply in the need to keep busy and avoid dealing with unpleasant issues. It can also be another cover-up for past or present emotional pain or a way to "hide" from troubled relationships. Whatever "fixing" purpose this private obsession serves, in the long run, it wreaks havoc in our lives.

HOOKED ON HURRY

Workaholism is closely related to what has been called "hurry sickness"—the urge not only to work continually, but to get everything done *quickly*. Not every workaholic has hurry sickness, but a great many do.

Do you recognize any of these symptoms?

- While on vacation: "Let's get this fishing out of the way."
- While lovemaking: Faster is better.
- While reading: "I've got to finish this novel by Monday."

For "hurrying" workaholics, life easily becomes a continuous uproar of completing one task after another, frantically seeking to avoid inactivity. Being "driven," after all, can happen in far more places than in the car! Time to eat? Every meal becomes fast food. Trying to communicate? Words are clipped and telegraphic.

"I'm a bottom-line person" you tell yourself, "I just don't have time to waste!" And somehow the real "bottom line" question— "Why am I hurrying?" never gets adequately answered.

Workaholics with hurry sickness, as a result, have a debilitating tendency to get nowhere—fast. They also become prime candidates for heart disease, strokes, and any number of stress-related illnesses.[1]

LEARNING TO TAKE IT EASY

Take a moment to consider the following workaholic tendencies. Do any of them sound like you?

- Are you "at work" (voluntarily) more than forty-five hours a week?
- Is the question, "Who are you?" answered by your profession?
- Do you tend to neglect your health or family because of work?
- Have you ever said, "my work is my play."
- Do you have trouble shutting off your mind in bed?
- Do you fill nonwork time (holidays, weekends) with work?
- Do you get nervous on vacation, finding it hard to "kick back" and relax?
- Has anyone close to you (not your boss!) accused you of working too hard?

If any of these apply to you, you may need to make a point of getting unhooked and learning how to rest.

---

1. See Hart, *Adrenalin and Stress,* 41–54 and Hart, *Healing Life's Hidden Addictions,* 171–89.

Why do you think God rested on the seventh day of creation? Was he stressed out? Overwhelmed? Burned out? I doubt it. He must have done it in order to demonstrate "rest" to this human race. And when we follow his example, we are both happier and more productive in the long run.

When I called a minister friend recently, I said, "Are you busy?"

"Yes," he replied. "I'm resting today." It was so refreshing to hear someone useful actually be unashamed to admit he was busy . . . resting.

I felt the same way when I heard actor Tom Selleck interviewed about what he would do after TV's "Magnum PI" series was over. He remarked, "I hope to have the courage to get off this roller coaster of activity. I'm afraid I'm addicted to the pace, and I want to get bored! I think I've been a little too goal-oriented; now I want to enjoy life." Good for you, Tom (you hunk)!

GETTING UNHOOKED

The ancient tale of the tortoise and the hare applies to us. Remember? The one with the slower, more steady (sane!) pace won the race. That's the goal for those of us who are hooked on hurry. We need to break free from our "drug of choice"—our work.

A career can be a source of great satisfaction, but it was never meant to be either a pain reliever or a constant source of stimulation. We use it that way at the cost of our physical, mental, and spiritual health.

That's what highly acclaimed Los Angeles news anchor Christine Lund found out. She spoke to a crowd of high achievers after suddenly resigning her high-visibility position due to workaholism. "I stand before you today as a contented 'fugitive from success,'" she stated with relief in her voice.

Now, breaking free of workaholism doesn't mean dumping our jobs and going on permanent leave! (Remember the compulsive person's "all or nothing" tendencies?) But it should aid us in setting some more realistic priorities.

My late, dear father-in-law, Dr. Herb Ezell, used to admonish me, "Learn to hurry without that hurried feeling." That's great advice. But for those of us with hurry sickness, it's easier said than done. I've discovered that it has to happen on the inside.

If you feel you may fall in the workaholic category, the "Stop! Look! Listen" process outlined in the chapters to come can be effective in helping you break free of your work obsession. In the meantime, consider the following specific hints:

- Schedule some time for rest and relaxation this week—keep reminding yourself, "My best requires rest."
- Ask those close to you, "Do you see me as a workaholic?" And then *listen* to what they have to say. (Remember, it is normal for people with hidden addictions to be in *denial*.)
- Repeat after me: "Becoming is more important than achieving—people are more important than projects." Try writing it in the front of your appointment book or posting it over your sink.
- Refuse to overschedule yourself—if necessary, block off an hour's "clear space" in every day's schedule to make room for problems and delays. Then work at accepting the fact that interruptions are a part of normal life.
- Try quitting "cold turkey." Deliberately avoid "time management" for twenty-four hours.
- Don't brag about the number of hours you put in on your job. If someone else praises you for overwork, make a point of reminding yourself that achievements and praise don't justify your being at work too much. (Try asking a trusted friend to make a point of praising you for *not* working!)
- Focus on learning to enjoy experiences and not just rewards. Begin to experience the journey and to enjoy the process.
- Most important, remind yourself over and over that your personal value is *not* dependent upon your life's work.

COMPULSIVE SHOPPING:
THE DESIRE TO ACQUIRE

As I have shown, workaholism can be extremely costly in terms of health and relationships. But compulsive shopping is costly in terms of finances as well! For millions of cash-and-credit-card-carrying women, the "urge to splurge" is irresistible. Studies show that 10 to 30 percent of the American population are shopaholics—people who shop compulsively to relieve inner distress.

"Get in Shape: SHOPPERCISE!" recommends an article in the November 1989 issue of *Redbook* magazine. Playing off the fact that such a large proportion of the American population is "out shopping," the writer advises readers to work exercise into their shopping trips. That means stretches to the high shelves, knee bends at the checkout counter, curled biceps in the tryout rooms. The theory is (apparently) that as you extend your shopping time, you can decrease your size simultaneously. (Just be careful when you try to pass by See's Candies!)

WHY MALL MANIA?

According to Dr. Georgia Witkin, author of *Quick Fixes and Small Comforts*, shopping is used for a variety of reasons: to kill time, to block upsetting thoughts, to boost self-esteem, or to escape loneliness. Shopping may be a way to fulfill a need for love, attention, or recognition, says Dr. Witkin.

For many of us, spending can be an unconscious form of compensation for a feeling of inferiority. ("A new outfit will surely cover *that* up . . .") We use spending binges to fill the emptiness in our lives. We spend to distract us from other problems; I know people who react to financial difficulties by going on shopping sprees!

Our materialistic culture is partly to blame for the prevalence of compulsive shopping as well. After all, we are constantly bombarded by advertisements assuring us that this dress (this car, this brand of mineral water) is all we need in order to be beautiful, happy, and fulfilled. No wonder that when we feel unhappy we assume that buying something will make us feel better!

At any rate, whatever the reasons, the cute bumper sticker slogan is all too true:

> **When the going gets tough,**
> **the tough go shopping.**

Unfortunately, shopping addictions can be emotionally and spiritually depleting, not to mention monetarily devastating. They can play havoc with relationships as well. Our friend Debi, whom we met earlier in the book, had this problem— and her shopping habit was gradually putting up a wall between her and her husband.

More important, like any addiction, shopping addictions are self-defeating. We go on shopping jags to cope with our feelings of emptiness. But can stuffing our arms with packages really fill our inner void?

If we were to analyze our shopping habits logically, many of us would have to say,

> **We crave things we don't**
> **need or enjoy.**
> **and we buy things we don't want**
> **to impress people we don't like.**

And like all addictions, instead of protecting us from our pain, our shopping addiction just brings more pain.

BEYOND THE MALLS

I've never struggled with being a "shopaholic," at least up to this point. Maybe that's because I'm more of a "borrowholic"; I enjoy wearing the glamorous clothes of my generous friends. For instance, I've attended three Presidential Inaugural Balls now—all with different elegant clothes—none of them my own!

One society-page reporter approached me in Washington, D.C., while I was wearing my friend Alyson's glittery blouse (again). The reporter, jotting her notes for the elite social pages, asked me, "Where did you get your outfit?"

"From Alyson's of Anaheim," I heard myself saying.

I saw it printed in the paper the next day. And I could imagine Southern California women, who let their fingers do the walking, scanning the yellow pages for Anaheim's exclusive (non-existent) shop "Alyson's of Anaheim."

However, although I cannot "'fess up" to having "mall mania," I do tend to be a mail-order-catalog freak. Somehow, when you don't even leave the privacy of your own home, you don't even feel like you're shopping! And when you simply copy down your credit-card number on an order form—or better yet, dial a toll-free number—it's easy to ignore the cost!

I've come to face the fact that growing up in "hand-me-downs" doesn't justify overspending now. I've had to call a halt to my secret shopping sprees in order to gain control over my shopping habit. Canceling those catalogues was painful but necessary. I've also confessed my weakness to a thoughtful friend, who keeps an eye on me (and on my doorstep for UPS packages!)

ARE YOU A SHOPPING JUNKIE?

Are you willing to examine your spending habits with the thought that you may have developed a private obsession with shopping? Maybe you're still in the "drooling over ads" stage. But beware—the next step is buying, not eying.

Here are some ways to tell you might be heading toward shopping addiction.

- Do you find yourself at the mall or shopping center (or reading mail-order catalogues) more than once a week?
- Do you ever find yourself buying something you hadn't planned to buy just "because it's bargain" or clipping coupons for items you ordinarily wouldn't consider buying?
- When you feel down or depressed, do you ever think of a shopping trip as a way to "cheer you up"?

- Do you keep a revolving balance on your credit cards?
- Do you ever bring a purchase home, only to find you already have the item or something very much like it?
- Do you usually come out of a store with more than you planned to buy?
- Do you have frequent arguments with your spouse or significant other about what you buy or the amounts you spend?
- Do you often bring home items for which you have no space?

A single yes answer to any of these questions does not make you a shopaholic, of course. But taken all together, positive responses to these questions may indicate a trend toward being hooked.

When considering whether or not you are hooked on shopping, don't be fooled into the trap of "I'm too broke to be a shopping addict"! The wealthy aren't the only ones hooked on shopping; they just indulge their addictions in more expensive places.

Contrary to popular opinion, the Bible doesn't say "Money is the root of all evil," but rather "the *love* of money is the root of all evil."[2] Curiously, when it comes to money and belongings, the folks who have the most money sometimes tend to belittle its value; it has ceased to be important to them. Instead, those who have the least often love money the most—and spend it appropriately.

OVERCOMING THE DESIRE TO ACQUIRE

Our shelf space, our closet space, and our attic and garage rafters tell on us. My friend, Jeanette, realizing she had a genuine "shoe fetish," announced to me,"I'm fasting shoes for the rest of this year." We can begin to cut off this "desire to acquire" at its root before it begins to grow "sucker shoots" and chokes the life out of us—and our budgets! As I have indicated, chapters 4 through 6 suggest a general process for

---

2. First Timothy 6:10, KJV, emphasis added.

breaking free of an addiction. But here are some additional, more specific suggestions for shopaholics:

- Plan ahead! Try to limit shopping trips to once or twice a week.
- Try to pinpoint the exact nature of your addiction and avoid that item. If you can't resist shoes, decide exactly which shoes you need and take someone with you to keep you out of trouble.
- When you go out to shop, write down the specific purpose (items) for which you are going.
- Shop in the appropriate department only; put your "store blinders" on!
- Extract the sale inserts from your newspaper ahead of time and throw them away.
- Beware of the "One Day Sale!"
- As you sit in the parking lot, before you enter a store, stop to remind yourself why you are there. If you can't justify your being there, say "no!" out loud and leave.
- If you've already bought something unnecessary, return it now. (If you feel intimidated, ask a friend to go along with you.) Don't wait, returning it will only become harder and harder.
- Don't be fooled by "good news mail"—"Instant Cash!" or "Enclosed is your preferred customer discount!" They are *advertisements,* not pennies from heaven!
- Beware of being an addictive coupon clipper!
- Don't rule out "drastic measures"—cutting up your credit cards, throwing away catalogues, hiring someone to shop for you, seeing a financial counselor.

ANALYSIS ADDICTION: HOOKED ON HEALING

As a spiritual counselor, I've talked to dozens of addicted women, and I've advised some of them to seek further advice. I obviously have nothing against counseling, therapy, or self-improvement—up to a point! But my experience in recent years has raised a serious concern in my mind about the dangers of some forms of counseling.

I have seen many a fine woman emotionally disabled and placed on the sidelines because she's been convinced by a counselor or some other purveyor of popular psychology that she is useless until she receives a form of "inner healing." As a result, many have become spiritual and emotional "MIAs," missing in the action of enjoying life and service to others.

The subject of "emotional healing" or "inner healing" is a current fad in the United States—popular in secular therapy, Christian circles, and other "spiritual" areas such as New Age. I trust the extreme emphasis on this form of healing—and its attendant dangers—will soon pass, leaving us with a nugget of truth.

Still, although the subject is a sacred cow to some people, as sociologist Tony Campolo put it, "sacred cows make great hamburgers." So let's dissect the subject together and free ourselves from what may be another private obsession.

The bookshelves are bulging with "self-awareness" books, and they sell well. Even in religious circles, many modern-day "theologians" (unfortunately, a lot of them are from my home state of California!) seem to be exporting a "doctrine of inadequacy" to all the world. Yet I believe both common sense and the Bible show clearly that too much focus upon self can render a person both psychologically and spiritually impotent. Self-indulgence, even when undertaken in a spirit of self-improvement, can be a debilitating disease. And self-analysis, undertaken for the wrong reasons and the wrong advice, can easily develop into a full-blown addiction.

For some reason, women seem to be especially vulnerable to the dangers of becoming advice junkies. It's no secret that women are the "main audience" for self-help products. We like Dial-a-Prayer, Dial-a-Shrink, Dial-a-Talk-Shows. And we seek counseling about even the most intimate details of our lives.

Our friend Clarice, introduced in chapter 2, had spun herself into a complex web of analysis addiction. Clarice was not a disabled VFW; she was a VIW, a Veteran of Internal Wars— and emotional gangrene was about to set in. Fortunately, she was delivered, but not without some significant setbacks.

What is the order of deterioration? Here's what I've seen. A woman . . .

- dedicates herself to delve deeply into her psyche (either to cope with painful circumstance or simply out of curiosity),
- becomes convinced that this must be an all-consuming search,
- renders herself incapable of caring for the needs of others (such as her family)—she must spend time on herself now,
- grows progressively self-absorbed, while relationships suffer, yet never seems to "get better."

Strangest of all, after having been immersed in psychology for years on end, the woman may eventually decide to become a counselor herself. Thus you'll find her registering for an unending curriculum of "psych" courses in her local school of ongoing education.

This kind of relentless trivial pursuit tends to motivate men and women to evaluate and analyze everyone they encounter—which often amounts to a form of judgmentalism and manipulation of others. Meanwhile, the past is never behind them, always in front of them. They are forever stumbling into new, unexplored territories of the inner person, beckoning them to continue the endless search. Unfortunately, they find that:

> **Emotional bingeing**
> **only leads**
> **to more hunger.**

Much of therapy is more observation than counseling. The patient has an opportunity to discharge her feelings, and that feels good. But venting emotions can become an addictive process in itself. In such a situation, the patient doesn't get well—only more dependent on the process of self-analysis.

Many of these analysis addicts may have been unfairly pigeonholed in the first place by some "therapist" and were stuffed into the "need emotional healing" category when their classification should have been: "problem not yet diagnosed." But regardless of the start of their problem, the result is the same: analysis addiction.

That's why the oft-quoted warning is so effective:

> **Beware of the paralysis**
> **of self-analysis.**

The Bible says it another way: "See to it that no one takes you captive through philosophy and empty deception. . . . These are matters which have, to be sure, the appearance of wisdom in self-made religion . . . but are of no value against fleshly indulgence."[3]

After my husband's first and second wives died, he got some very valuable advice. His physician friend warned him to remember how a wound heals; it forms a scab. If we continue picking at that scab, we risk infection and delayed healing.

Now, I am *not* saying we should ignore the past. In fact, there is great benefit in reviewing the past in order to remove obstacles and hindrances to freedom—the healing process I outline in chapters to come will offer an opportunity to do just that. But the fact remains that we will never be able to rewrite the original script of childhood, no matter how many times we force ourselves to review it. It's "in the can," as they say in the film industry—*done*. No amount of digging will change what has happened. The only point in examining the past, therefore, is in changing the negative effect our past may be having on the present. And doing that does *not* require a lifetime of analysis.

GROUP ANALYSIS ADDICTION

In the 20 February 1989 edition of *Newsweek* magazine, dealing with the subject of support groups, actor Tony Curtis expressed his vision of the support groups of the future: "Instead of having bars on every few blocks, we should have

---

3. Colossians 2:8, 23.

little therapy centers where you can pull your car over and have a chance to talk to somebody."

I have a friend who has a black belt in therapy groups! She has expertly developed the art of hiding in these groups and "swapping" addictions with other members, even occasionally "trading up."

Therapy groups, in other words, can be just another form of the same addiction. That doesn't mean that groups are bad in themselves. Seeking support in friendships, fellowship communities, and—yes—specific support groups can be vital to recovering from a private obsession. I even recommend finding or starting such a group in a later chapter.

But the very effectiveness of support groups makes them an especially fertile breeding ground for dependencies. Since the support of others can make us feel so good, it is easy to get hooked on the warmth of group dynamics. And when the group starts serving the purpose of fixing our feelings rather than helping us face them, the addictive process is fueled.

In addition, the "fad" nature of therapy groups makes them especially conducive to addiction. Looking back, it seems to me that every decade seems almost marked with its own brand of addictive revelation:

- 1960s—Rebellion (against authority)
- 1970s—Empowerment (drugs, feminism, etc.)
- 1980s—The ME Generation (yuppies, consumerism)
- 1990s—The WE Generation (support groups)

THE DISABLING DILEMMA

Where does analysis addiction begin? I have watched countless women eagerly walk into seminars seeking encouragement, only to limp out, convinced they will remain emotionally crippled unless they receive therapeutic help. In almost every case, the sponsor of the seminar, aware of his clients' vulnerability, just happened to offer a counseling plan that the woman could buy into "if you're searching for a useful, productive life."

How sad! A supposed "expert" in the field of therapy authoritatively tells these women, "There is something *very* wrong. Somewhere in your past, though you are not consciously aware of it, an unknown event is disabling you. You *must* begin in-depth therapy to unearth this as-yet-unidentified experience." Immediately the imagination (the "vain" imagination, as the Bible calls it!) goes to work:

- Is my father my real father?
- Was I sexually abused and don't remember it? If so, who abused me? Uncle Jack? Aunt Ethel?
- Did Mom impose cruel and unusual punishment upon me?

Once we begin struggling with an unknown past, it is psychologically possible to "conjure up" all sorts of possibilities. We become lost in a labyrinth of "maybe . . ." "where?" "who?" and "how?" In this soap-opera ritual, we seek to come out of the "Dark Shadows" into a "Brighter Day." The problem is, this sort of intense introspection can lead us into "Another World" or—worse yet—"General Hospital!"

I am sorry to say that I have repeatedly seen this destructive technique used on dedicated women who desire to serve God in helping others. The hook used to sway the potential counselee in this case is, "You know, you can't be used to heal others until you're healed yourself."

It is unfortunate that many folks privately cultivate a secret fear, inspired by an accusing voice inside that says, "Something is wrong with you! You need help. You can't put your finger on it, but until you do, you must diligently search within, probing the depths of your psyche. Until you discover 'IT' you are out of commission—no good to God, yourself, or others."

It is also unfortunate that many well-meaning counselors make their living off this accusing voice. They willingly agree that the client must commit herself, exclusively, to excavating this elusive "root problem." *What a disabling, deceptive dilemma!*

This expedition into the regions beyond our reach is too often futile, leaving the explorers sapped of motivation and

confidence—convinced they are spiritually handicapped. All
the inward probing leaves them little time to look around and
see the needs of others. But what difference does it make? By
now the searchers are convinced that they don't have anything
to offer the world anyway.

ARE YOU A VICTIM OF ANALYSIS ADDICTION?

Are you a victim of the analysis trap? Have you let your
yearning for wholeness develop into a dependency on navel
gazing? Here are some possible indications this may be true:

- Do you find yourself buying book after book, listening to
  broadcast after broadcast, or attending multiple seminars
  on psychological wholeness?
- Do you tend to "feel better" the minute you get in your
  therapist's office or settle down with a self-help book or
  tape?
- Does your family complain about the time you spend
  trying to "find yourself" and "find healing"?
- Have you been in ongoing counseling or a therapy group
  for more than six months?
- Do you tend to change counselors/groups periodically in
  the hopes of finding one that works for you? How long
  ago did you begin this trend?
- Has anyone ever observed that, in spite of your efforts at
  self-analysis, you're not getting better?
- Do you tend to have difficulty coping if you miss a
  counseling or group session?
- Do you tend to put off dealing with certain issues "until I
  get better" or avoid activities because "I can't help
  anyone else until I take care of me"?
- Do you believe there is something subconsciously wrong
  with you and that you cannot be happy until you discover it?

A CALL FOR COMMON SENSE

In this morass of probing and analysis, we desperately need
a word of common sense. Yes, our past can influence us. Yes,

we all may need some form of inner healing. I wouldn't be writing this book if that were not true.

But no! The vast majority of us do not need to spend large chunks of our time in self-analysis—nor do we need to be totally "healed" before we can be useful or worthwhile. And even "sane" therapy is not the total answer for our deepest needs or the real source of our healing.

I myself was raised in a classic "dysfunctional home" in an inner-city neighborhood in Philadelphia. Both my parents were alcoholics. My father told me, point blank, that he'd never wanted me (I was supposed to be "Lee, the boy.") The middle child of five girls, I was battered and abused by him, as were my sisters and mother. Like so many others, I never heard the words "I love you" from either of my parents. Deprived of affection and receiving only physical abuse at home, my "father image" was destroyed.

After becoming a Christian at age seventeen at a Billy Graham Crusade, I left home as a virgin teenager, only to be raped on my first office job in California. This sexual abuse resulted in pregnancy, and this "unwanted child" gave birth to an "unplanned child" in a Los Angeles County Facility. I released my tiny daughter—the only child I would ever give birth to—for adoption. (These events are chronicled in my book, *The Missing Piece.*[4])

Due to my mistrust of men, I waited until I was twenty-eight to marry. My husband, Hal, a widower, made me an instant mother in marriage; I adopted his two wonderful daughters, Pamela and Sandra. These girls were also bruised children. Having survived the tragic deaths of two mothers, they were understandably reluctant to trust me, the candidate for Mother #3. Quite a novice, I diligently practiced "mothering" on these dear girls, giving them all I had to offer at the time.

Through my personal circumstances as a "victim," I came to understand that only God could provide the power to heal me on the inside. No, he didn't instantly zap me from above with a heavenly bolt of healing. But as I learned to look to him, to trust him, to believe he was able to give me what I

4. Lee Ezell, *The Missing Piece* (New York: Bantam, 1988).

needed, the healing came. And as I traveled on the road to healing, I was able to help others as well.

The spiritual journey on which God led me included surrender, forgiveness, and "restoring my soul." As Psalm 23 records, the Lord *was* my Shepherd. I did not want. He led me. He fed me. He stuck with me. Because of what he did for me, *I am emotionally finished with my past.* No continuous review and analysis are required.

THE PATH TO INNER HEALING

Let me assure you that I have been worked over by many who were caught up in a private obsession with analysis. These people can't believe I can be honestly healthy and useful without probing through the rubble of my past with a therapist as my guide. They can only conclude that I must be in "denial"—yes, that's it, denial! Although I appear to be doing all right, my happiness is surely a cover-up for a need of which I am unaware. (In this way, a true and useful insight—the fact of denial—becomes a manipulative tool—the accusation of denial.)

Obviously, I can't *prove* I'm not in denial. And as I've already confessed, my life today isn't devoid of problems. But I'm basically happy. I'm whole. I'm fulfilled. My past circumstances aren't crippling my present life.

And that's why I can say, from experience, that:

> **God will give you**
> **what you need**
> **when you need it.**

Do you feel you need help? Do your homework, research sources of help, then relax. I am convinced that the "Wonderful Counselor," the "Prince of Peace,"[5] can gently give you direction to discover the root of your problem, speak with a

5. Isaiah 9:6.

friend, find the right counselor, or even locate a helpful support group.

Whatever you do, don't become hooked on a quest for some damaging past experience buried in your psyche. There are so many psychological swamps out there—many people have been swallowed up in the alluring mire of therapy and never returned to usefulness in life. They become engulfed in self-indulgence, unable to function.

Instead of getting hooked on therapy, focus on your spiritual quest. Permit God to reveal all things to you at the right time (he may or may not use other people in the process.) I am convinced you will discover this truth:

Strengthening our weak spiritual life gives us access to what we really need to break free of private obsessions.

My friend Don Stephens is Youth with a Mission's director of the mercy ship *Anastasis*, bringing disaster relief and mercy to third-world nations. I remember the puzzled look on his face when I asked him what he thought of emotional healing.

"Emotional healing?" he repeated, "what *is* it?"

"Never mind," I replied to this statesman of caring, who carries a mobile "Mother Teresa" ministry to thousands worldwide. I knew he could never be rendered "out of service" by the paralysis of self-analysis.

"Never mind," I chuckled. "This, too, shall pass!"

Even without the availability of a licensed therapist, I believe it is possible for anyone with a painful or dysfunctional past to find peace and satisfaction.

And I certainly believe it is possible to break free of any private obsession, including the treacherous trio of workaholism, shopaholism, and analysis addiction. My own healing came from walking through the simple strategies I will outline in the next three chapters. This recovery plan is also my maintenance program for continuing contentment. It works!

breaking free from private obsessions

5

stop!

a screeching halt

An "ancient" proverb, immortalized by contemporary author Jamie Buckingham, says:

> **The truth will set you free;**
> **but first**
> **it will make you miserable!**

Unpleasant as it can be, daring to discover the truth about ourselves is the first step to realizing what freedom truly is.

I applaud you for continuing your reading this far; it should be an encouraging sign for you. You want to change. You have a desire to do things differently, and this is commendable! Once you admit you have a private obsession, then you have the option for recovery.

Uh-oh. Are you beginning too feel butterflies in your stomach? Good! Let's show them how to fly in formation!

TAMING THE TIGER

Remember those old gasoline commercials that suggested, "Put a tiger in your tank?" Well, we all seem to have two tigers inside us. One is there for good, the other for evil. As wild creatures will do, they appear to be fighting all the time. And you know which one is winning? *The one you feed the most!*

That's why it's important to starve out that addictive personality inside us and to feed the spiritual side of us, preparing ourselves to win the battle. If we don't, our willpower will suffer from iron-deficiency anemia, and we'll find ourselves on the verge of spiritual malnutrition!

Let's put aside our excuses, then, and expose them for what they are. Once we realize that the following statements simply *explain* our behavior, maybe we'll be able to stop using them to *excuse* our behavior.

- "I'm only human."
- "Hey, if _____ is my worst vice, I'm lucky."
- "I have no willpower."
- "I just can't face it right now; I'll handle it later."
- "There is nothing I can do."
- "My behavior is controlled by past events in my life."
- "I shouldn't have to struggle to get over this; it'll come."
- "If I genuinely want something, I should be able to have it."
- "It's not that big a deal."
- "I *need* it now; I'll deal with the problems it causes later."
- "I'll feel better afterward."
- "This is *me*, like it or not"
- "I'm worthless; it doesn't matter anyhow."
- "I've failed before, and this probably won't be the last time."
- "I am a failure."

THE STRUGGLE FOR FREEDOM

We could perhaps picture better the power of our private obsession if we thought of it in this way. A terrorist has come aboard and hijacked your life! He has taken over the controls of your will, and you are going to have to break into that cockpit and wrestle with him for control. This terrorist's name is *habit.* And, if you are striving for personal growth and maturity, you are determined to rule your life's destination by your own choices, not by habits. Right?

Right! We must *stop* this misdirected flight and regain control!

Remember—any skill we have learned and practiced will soon become a habit. Some habits are good. They help us use our brains for other, more constructive projects. But other habits act like parasites—they give us a quick "high," use up all our energy getting there, and then let us come back down—Whoomp!—exhausted and regretful.

We are empowered by the right choices.
We are weakened by the wrong choices.

By gaining self-control, we establish new habit patterns. And remember, *why* we decide to do something is more important that *what* we decide to do. We will be taking a closer look at this reality in the chapters to follow.

Here's another reality: If you want to change how you *feel,* you've got to change how you *act.* Then you need to hold to that new action until acting in a healthy manner becomes just as comfortable as acting in a compulsive manner used to be. The good news is that if you can go thirty days without giving in, your chances of conquering your addiction will increase markedly and the strength of its obsessive power will diminish.

But don't worry about the thirty days. Just think about *now.* And starting where you are, resolve to take *one day at a time!*

DOING OUR PART

As I have indicated, the most effective approach to developing self-control is a spiritual one. It involves depending on a Higher Power, whom I know as God, for help. But what is our part in all this? It includes the care and feeding of that good life, from God, that lies within each of us. Then, when we take the step to do the natural, God will do the supernatural.

Doing our part does not magically produce the inner change we desire, but it puts us in a place where change can occur. Doing our part qualifies us to receive the help we need.

> **We cannot do what God must do;**
> **God will not do what we must do.**

TWELVE STEPS TO FREEDOM

As I indicated in an earlier chapter, the Twelve-Step program used by Alcoholics Anonymous and its sister recovery groups has proven remarkably effective against the devastation of addiction. These steps, which are essentially a spiritual approach, are:

THE TWELVE STEPS OF ALCOHOLICS ANONYMOUS

1. We admitted we were powerless over alcohol—that our lives had become unmanageable.
2. We came to believe that a Power greater than ourselves could restore us to sanity.
3. We made a decision to turn our will and our lives over the care of God as we understood him.
4. We made a searching and fearless moral inventory of ourselves.
5. We admitted to God, to ourselves, and to another human being the exact nature of our wrongs.
6. We were entirely ready to have God remove all these defects of character.
7. We humbly asked God to remove our shortcomings.
8. We made a list of all persons we had harmed and became willing to make amends to them all.
9. We made direct amends to such people wherever possible, except when to do so would injure them or others.

10. We continued to take personal inventory and when we were wrong promptly admitted it.

11. We sought through prayer and meditation to improve our conscious contact with God as we understood him, praying only for knowledge of his will for us and the power to carry that out.

12. Having had a spiritual awakening as the result of these steps, we tried to carry this message to alcoholics, and to practice these principles in all our affairs.[1]

A THREE-PART STRATEGY

I find it helpful to break these Twelve Steps down into three general strategies or steps which I sum up as:

- STOP! (AA Steps 1–3)
- LOOK! (AA Steps 4–8)
- LISTEN! (AA Steps 9–12)

I believe the basic direction of these three steps can also be summed up in this encouraging Bible verse from Hebrews 12:1:

- STOP!   "Let us lay aside every weight . . .
- LOOK!   . . . and the sin which so easily besets us . . .
- LISTEN!   . . . and let us run with patience the race set before us . . ."

A STRATEGY FOR THE WHOLE PERSON

We humans are distinguished above other species by our complex threefold nature; we are made up of:

- body (our physical nature),
- soul (including our mind, will, and emotions), and
- spirit (that inner, immortal spark that can "know God").

---

1. Reprinted with permission of Alcoholics Anonymous, World Services, Inc.

To be effective, therefore, recovery must touch all areas of our lives. It must involve physical actions. It must call for the participation of our thoughts, feelings, and determination. And it must involve a relationship and dependence on God.

The three steps or strategies for recovery do just that:

- STOP! Involves the *physical* action of ceasing the compulsive behavior, as well as understanding how physical needs can complicate the compulsive process and recognizing our physical limitations—we can't overcome an addiction alone.
- LOOK! Involves examining the ways our past experiences and feelings affect our actions and taking steps to develop our *mental and emotional* capabilities.
- LISTEN! Involves reaching for the *spiritual* support you need (both from God and other people) to keep on overcoming.

READY, SET, *STOP* . . . FOR A MOMENT OF TRUTH

In identifying a private obsession and overcoming it, the obvious first step is to STOP! And the first STOP we should make is to face some realities about ourselves and our behavior. We must admit that our compulsive behavior is damaging us in some way and therefore make the decision to cease our participation in whatever it is. The shopaholic decides to stop reading sale ads; the compulsive eater resolves to stop eating between meals; the compulsive house cleaner determines to stop searching for another area to be scrubbed.

The first step to breaking any private obsession is to STOP and analyze, in a much needed moment of truth: "Are these things true of me?"

- I see my activity as potentially self-destructive.
- I recognize I have an addiction to it.
- I admit I am powerless over it.
- I got myself into this mess, but I cannot get myself out.

Now, take heart, and repeat after me...

- I will STOP procrastinating.
- I will STOP hoping the problem will get better.
- I will STOP my denial.
- I am so sorry for the way I've allowed this problem to develop in my life.
- I am in need of help, God.

In Bible talk, making that "STOP" decision means you are "repenting." And that simply means you are in the process of turning around. You've admitted your powerlessness and failure; you want help so you can really change.

STOP YOUR ACTIONS

After you have agreed to STOP and seen the need to STOP, don't waste that miracle! Follow it with action. Stop your next compulsive behavior, whatever it is. Don't worry about whether you will be able to stop the habit completely. "Just say no" the next time the urge strikes.

Stopping at this point has all sorts of implications. You may need to *STOP at the thought stage.* When your mind begins to play that "you need this now" trick on you, speak out loud and tell yourself "STOP!" When your mind begins to wander off again to that old, comfortable, warming thought, catch it before it materializes into action.

You'll also want to *STOP the cues* that trigger your addictive response. What gives you the "cue" to behave in a certain way? What "goes together"? Coffee and a cigarette? A sale ad and a credit card purchase? Get rid of whatever tempts you to give in to compulsive behavior—paraphernalia, that magazine, that tempting food.

You will almost certainly have to *STOP feeding the habit.* Realize that "just one phone call" will lead to another. One more romance novel will make the next one harder to resist.

To STOP may mean to throw out—

- a magazine,
- a book,
- a meeting announcement.

To STOP may mean to refuse—

- some interrupting noise (TV, music),
- some sort of entertainment,
- a sport activity,
- another counseling session.

To STOP may mean to deny yourself—

- another lottery ticket,
- another romance novel,
- keeping up with the soaps,
- one more phone call.

To STOP may mean to come out—

- out of that unhealthy relationship,
- "out of hiding" through confession,
- out of depression to walk in the light.

DEBI

Debi and Dennis had just spent three days trying to figure some way to get through an overwhelming financial crisis. Their credit-card debt had topped fifteen thousand dollars, and they were more than sixty days late on some of their payments. Should they borrow from their parents? Refinance their home? Should Debi get a job? How could they escape from their terrible financial straits?

After hours of tearful conversations, shouted accusations, and reluctant confessions, Debi had slowly come to realize that she was, by and large, responsible for the problems they faced. She had been willful, selfish, and—yes—compulsive with her shopaholic habits.

The next morning, as Debi puttered around the house, she heard the thud of the mail in the box. As she looked through it, she felt a shiver of delight when she discovered the mailman had delivered four brand new catalogs—including her very favorites, Tweeds® and J. Crew®—both on the same day! Debi could hardly wait to sit down with a cup of herb tea and order "just a little something to cheer me up."

Then she remembered.

She thought about the mountain of bills in the kitchen drawer, and she sadly recalled Dennis's puzzled face as he searched his brain for a way to pay them. She had promised him, very sincerely, that she would no longer spend money without his approval. And, she knew all too well, there was no way on earth he was going to approve of a new Tweeds turtleneck or a J. Crew dress to be crammed into her already bulging closet!

Debi's mind wandered to her crystals, and to the "inner voice" she'd often heard, encouraging her to please herself and to have what she wanted. At this point, she wasn't so sure it was a voice to which she should listen again. She shook her head grimly as she headed for the trash can with the catalogs.

"God, help me!" she said out loud as she closed the lid on the kitchen trash can. "I've got to change my bad habits. I mean it, God. If you're there, I need your help. I can't do it by myself!"

STOP FOR A PERIOD OF TIME

When I think of STOP, I think of calling a *fast* in my activity.

In its strictest meaning, of course, fasting means to abstain from food—usually for spiritual purposes—for a specified period of time.

If we are compulsive overeaters, then literal fasting—even for one meal—is an excellent way to stop that particular compulsion. But "fasting" from other compulsive behaviors can be equally effective. Perhaps we need to call a fast from scanning sale catalogs, from TV, from spending money, from relationships—any activity which triggers our compulsiveness.

It won't be easy. Let's face it, any kind of fasting is a battle. Like a spoiled child, your stomach will begin to grumble and give you a hard time when it doesn't get the food it wants when it wants it. The same is true of any "cold turkey" change of habit!

The "period of time" idea of fasting is especially important here. Why not just say, "I'm stopping forever"? Because you'll be overwhelmed. You "know," deep down inside, that you don't have what it takes, by yourself, to give up your compulsive behavior—if you did, you wouldn't be addicted in the first place!

But "fasting for a period of time" makes stopping seem "doable." We may not be able to STOP forever, but we can "fast" for a limited period of time. And that "fasting" period will:

- strengthen your confidence,
- give you time to build your spiritual resources,
- give you emotional space to look at your compulsive behavior honestly and ask for help,
- distinguish more clearly between your desires and your needs.

STOP CONFUSING DESIRE WITH NEED

One of the realities that STOPPING helps us internalize is that:

```
A desire

is not a

mandate.
```

"I just *have to* talk to someone," contends the Telephone Junkie (for the ninth time that day).

"I've *got to* offer to be cookie chairman," volunteers the already overtaxed Supermom. "What'll the PTA think of me if I don't?"

"Oh, I *must keep* that vase," surrenders the Pack Rat. "I can give it as a gift if I can't find space in the garage."

"I've *got to* stay here with the cats. Nobody else knows how they like their food," rationalizes the Pet Freak.

"But I *need* another pair of silver lamé pumps with sequined inserts," moans the Shopaholic.

One of the basic truths our addictions keep us from seeing is that there is a difference between our desires and our needs. Needs are necessities; desires are wants. The credit card abuser doesn't "need" that new item American Express offered him, although he feels like he can't leave home without it!

Now, it's easy to play mind games here about certain private obsessions. Obviously, for example, we need food; we need sleep. But we don't need to overeat or stuff ourselves between meals or mainline chocolate! We don't need to nap whenever we feel a crisis coming on! We become compulsive overeaters or nappers not because we need food or sleep, but because we desire the comfort or relief that certain forms of eating or sleeping bring us.

Now, I don't want to imply that life has to be just a grim process of obtaining the bare necessities of existence—scrabbling for the basics of food and shelter with no joy, no delight, no extras. God never said we should not have desires. In fact, he has made an incredible promise regarding our desires:

> **Delight yourself in the Lord;
> and *He* will give you the
> desires of your heart.** [2]

Wow, doesn't that sound like a gold mine? Yes, but note what it says. Not, "You should have anything you want because you deserve it." Not "go for the gusto." It says, "God will give you everything you desire, but only as part of the process of getting to know God."

We need to so "delight ourselves" in God, that soon we are willing to allow him to *put his desires* into our hearts. When he puts desires in our hearts, he also provides the fulfillment—the joy, the delight, the extras.

---

2. Psalms 37:4, emphasis added.

And part of that process of changing our desires is to learn the difference between our own desires and our genuine needs. Here are three helpful sentences we can say to ourselves when tempted:

- "I do not really *need* this, although I'd really like to have it" (or do it).
- "I will wait a day or two and see just how badly I want it then."
- "I will pray that if this is not right for me, God will STOP the feeling of longing."

STOP LETTING CIRCUMSTANCES DICTATE YOUR BEHAVIOR

Sometimes outside and inside circumstances such as physical needs and emotional conditions can affect the way we make decisions and can hinder us from making the right ones. We long for external validation when we don't feel good about ourselves, and at times we lose track of what is causing our sense of deprivation.

Because that is true, the AA program has another excellent standard with which to measure when to STOP. They call it H.A.L.T.

The idea, when you feel compelled to indulge in unhealthy behavior is to ask yourself a simple question about your overall physical or emotional state:

> "Am I . . . **H**ungry
> **A**ngry
> **L**onely or
> **T**ired?"

Then, be kind to yourself. Deal with the overall condition. But no matter what you are up against, don't allow yourself to be backed against a wall by things you can control. When you feel yourself falling into your compulsive behavior and you recognize one of these complications, do something about it. Be on guard!

When you've gone too long without eating, you're going to feel the "need" for some sort of satisfaction. H.A.L.T! Get something healthy to eat, or just recognize that dinner is in an hour and you can wait.

When you sense anger boiling inside you, you'd better confess it, or it will remain buried alive and drive you toward addictive behavior. H.A.L.T. Talk out the anger, or write it out.

When loneliness wants to overtake you and push you from your pity party to the mall, a box of chocolate, or anyone's arms, H.A.L.T.! Call a friend. Write a letter. Plan a strategy for meeting people. Or just recognize that everyone feels lonely sometimes and that your loneliness is probably temporary.

When you are overtired, depression is just around the corner. H.A.L.T.! Take a break, or a walk, or a short nap.

It's possible to play mind games here, too. If your private obsession is with the telephone, for example, recognizing you're lonely is *not* reason for another marathon Sprint® session. The point of H.A.L.T. is to enable you to recognize and cope with outside pressures that may push you into compulsive behavior—not give you excuses for that behavior.

Instead of falling into that trap, let's make a serious, honest commitment to STOP . . . and H.A.L.T. . . . and prepare ourselves for spiritual growth.

STOP TO FACE THE TRUTH ABOUT GOD AND YOURSELF

The A.A. Twelve Steps center on developing wellness by inviting God to join in the healing process. I am convinced that approach is the only key to lasting and positive change.

But perhaps you have already been praying to a God who is apparently not hearing you. You're still struggling, even though you've already told God what's wrong and what he needs to do about it.

Perhaps the problem is that you've asked for God's help without turning control of the situation over to him. Are you still trying to handle things on your own without depending on God's help? If so, you're going to need to STOP and face some truths about yourself and about God. Truths regarding your own limitations, God's power, and the need to ask for help.

Regardless of where you are coming from, when it comes to dealing with God, you're going to have to surrender your self-will. Otherwise, you'll expect everyone—including God—to act in a manner which pleases you. Let's accept the fact that we may not know what is best for us in every situation. Let's let go of our unanswered questions, and our broken dreams:

BROKEN DREAMS

As children bring their broken toys
with tears for us to mend,
I brought my broken dreams to God
because he was my friend.
But then, instead of leaving him
in peace to work alone,
I hung around and tried to help
with ways that were my own.
At last, I snatched them back and cried,
"How can you be so slow?"
"My child," he said,
"What could I do?
You never did let go."

—Author Unknown

It bears repeating: surrendering our self-will is necessary before we can fully put ourselves in the hands of God. Self-will tries to convince us that we are on our own and that we have all the answers. Not so! Our very evident powerlessness over private obsessions should be proof enough of our personal ability to solve problems! No matter what the circumstances, we need a resource greater than ourselves that we can turn to.

Now, that doesn't mean we have to have all the answers about God or even be completely convinced before we can receive help. And it certainly doesn't mean that having all the answers releases us from the need to give in to God. No matter where we are in our journey of belief, we are all basically in the same spiritual boat: Living healthy, sane, and productive lives requires surrendering our will to Someone greater than we are. Pulling ourselves up by our own boot-straps is against the law of gravity. To move higher up, we must have a grip on a solid object that is higher than ourselves.

If, at this point, you don't have a personal faith, your willingness will do for now. As you continue to grow, as you see the results of surrendering to God's help, I'm convinced your faith will grow.

Are you open to discover the reality of a God-power? If you can turn on the light switch and enjoy the light without understanding how electricity works, then why can't you also accept and enjoy the existence of a Power you don't under-stand? And if he should happen to exist, would you be willing to give him the opportunity to help you? That's all you need to start.

All of us must be willing to STOP believing that we are our own higher power. And once we've given up that responsibil-ity, we can also stop endlessly talking to ourselves and scold-ing ourselves. We can begin talking to God—he's been listen-ing all the while. Be assured that you won't surprise or shock him with your revelations. He already knows what's going on! He's been wanting you to wake up and to turn to him for the help he's extending your way.

If God has seemed to disappoint you, I encourage you to reexamine the terms on which we inhabit this planet. This world is not a well-run kindergarten where the good are always rewarded and the bad are always punished. Let's adjust our concept of God to reality. We will not be able to worship a disappointing God. And bad things do, unfortu-nately, happen to good people in this imperfect world. But people good and bad are also granted the spiritual power to grow and to overcome setbacks through their dependence on the God of love and power.

STOP AND CONSIDER THE CLAIMS OF CHRIST

I can vividly recall the night I surrendered my broken dreams to God and gained a more accurate picture of who the Higher Power really is. As I mentioned before, it happened to me when I was attending a Billy Graham Crusade as a teen-ager. I figured it was some kind of a holy-roller meeting and was curious to see what would happen there.

I was pleasantly surprised to discover quite a normal-looking crowd gathered to hear Dr. Graham's lecture. As I listened, I realized how nebulous my understanding of God really was. That night I surrendered my life to Jesus Christ, receiving him as my own Savior. Without this spiritual infusion of power, I could never have made it through the rape and subsequent pregnancy that occurred just a year later. I have tested this "life in Christ" against some powerful odds and its validity has been proven to me again and again.

You will note that I said, "in Christ." My faith hinges on my belief that I come to the "Higher Power" through the person of Jesus Christ. Now this poses a difficulty for some people, even some who accept the idea of a "superior being."

Many folks are willing to acknowledge that Christ was a great moral teacher and a good example to be followed, but they stumble when it comes to accepting Christ's claim to be God. Yet the classic author C. S. Lewis disarms us with his ever-clear thinking:

> A man who was merely a man, and said the sort of things Jesus said would not be a great moral teacher. He would either be a lunatic, or else he would be the devil of hell. You must make your choice. Either this man was, and is, the Son of God; or else a madman, or something worse. But let us not come with any patronising nonsense about his being a great human teacher. He has not left that open to us. He did not intend to.[3]

_____

3. C. S. Lewis, *Mere Christianity* (New York: Macmillan, 1952), 56.

Christ did not shy away from claiming, as recorded in the Gospel of John, "He who has seen Me has seen the Father." He also said, "No one comes to the Father, but through Me."[4] In our own terms, this can only be translated, "No one comes to the Higher Power, except by me." These claims are either intolerably arrogant, absolutely nuts, or unequivocally true!

So, the gauntlet is thrown at our feet. Was Christ a deceiver? A madman? Or the Jewish Messiah? What do you think?

That's the question I urge you, above all, to STOP and consider.

----

4. John 14:6, 9.

self-test #3
coming to grips with God

Having acknowledged your private obsession, your power-lessness over it, and your need for a power greater than yourself, thoughtfully answer the following questions:

1. Do you believe a Higher Power (God) exists?
    ____ Yes ____ No

2. Do you believe the wonders of nature reveal the exist-ence of God (general revelation)? ____ Yes ____ No

3. Does it make sense to you that God would create the world and then abandon it, exercising no control or influence over it? ____ Yes ____ No

4. If God is involved in the world, doesn't it also make sense that he would make himself known to his creation (special revelation)? ____ Yes ____ No

5. God claims he has made himself known by his special revelation to humankind, the Bible. Do you believe that? ____ Yes ____ No

6. The focus of the Bible—the center of God's special revelation—is the person of Christ. Do you believe he existed? ____ Yes ____ No

7. Jesus claimed to be the Son of God. Based on C. S. Lewis's argument, do you think his claims were ____ True ____ False?
    If false, do you think he knew they were false?
    ____ Yes ____ No.

If they were false, and he knew they were false, he was a liar. If they were false, and he didn't know they were false, he was insane. If his claims are true—he is the God-Man!

8. As the God-Man, do you believe Christ came, as he said he did, to pay the price (death) for man's self-centered rebellion (sin) against God? ____ Yes ____ No

9. Do you believe Christ died on the cross as payment for your sin? ____ Yes ____ No

10. Do you accept that you will never be "good enough" to pay for your sin with your "good works," that Christ's death is the only acceptable price? ____ Yes ____ No

11. Are you ready to let Christ pay for your sin and stop trying to pay for it yourself? ____ Yes ____ No

12. Do you want to have a personal relationship with God through Christ his Son? ____ Yes ____ No

God has given us his revelation, and he waits patiently for us to respond to his revealed truth. You can do that now by praying—simply talking to God. Agree with God about your self-centered rebellion (confess your sin to him) and accept Christ's payment for it on the cross (believe in Christ). Having received Christ as your Savior, you have opened the door to a deep relationship with him. This beginning step is further enhanced by reading the Bible and seeking out friendship with others who want to deepen their contact with God.

Don't worry if you don't "feel" changed yet. It isn't what you feel that counts now; it is the fact that your faith can grow. The Higher Power is real, and you have said yes to him. That means that, whatever you might feel at the moment, you have taken the first steps toward coming to grips with God!

6

---

look!

inward and upward

OK! Let's take a look at where we are in the STOP, LOOK, and LISTEN recovery plan.

We've decided to STOP whatever it is we've been doing obsessively. We've admitted that we're not exactly thrilled with certain habits or with other particular aspects of our personalities. And we've made the decision to STOP fooling ourselves into thinking we can handle it own our own—we've turned to God for help.

But stopping our unhealthy behavior is not enough. We know we can only hold out for so long, and we've already admitted we'll need a good deal more than willpower. Stopping can temporarily control our compulsive behavior, but will do nothing to resolve the inner problem that caused the compulsion in the first place.

A successful journey out of the land of addiction begins with a willingness to do whatever it takes to expose and deal with the cause, rather than enacting temporary abstinence. And that's why it's time to take another step.

It's time to LOOK—

- at ourselves,
- at those around us, and
- at God—

for understanding of the past, for present peace, and for future hope.

CLARICE

Bud walked in the house and slammed the door. "Listening to the radio again?" He commented to Clarice, who was shocked to see him home at four in the afternoon.

"Oh . . . I didn't know you'd be home so early, Bud." She quickly snapped off the radio and carried a half-eaten piece of cake into the kitchen. She could almost feel Bud's disapproval, and was embarrassed that he'd caught her snacking. *I've got to stop overeating! I hate this feeling of being caught!*

"Clarice, I want to talk to you about something."

"Not the 'self-centered' lecture again, I hope," she scowled defensively.

"No, it's something else. I've been thinking a lot about the things you do that bother me, Clarice. And I want to apologize for being so critical." His voice had lowered and softened.

"Excuse me?" *He's up to something!* Clarice thought to herself. *Surely I haven't been misjudging him!*

"I said I want to apologize. Look, I know you think I'm kind of a loser as a Christian, Clarice. And I'll admit I'm not much of a churchgoer. But I've got this idea lately, and I'm not sure God isn't the One giving it to me. I even left work early today to talk to you about it."

"What's your idea?"

"That the reason you're always eating and listening to all that religious stuff on the radio and tapes is because you've got some hurts you're hiding from." To her amazement, Bud reached over and took her hand unexpectedly. Her eyes teared up. Before she knew it, she was crying.

"Clarice, if I'm the one causing you pain, I want to know what it is I'm doing wrong."

The two looked at each other for a long time. "Well," she finally said, "For one thing, you don't seem very interested in talking to me anymore."

"Go on. . . ."

"Well, it kind of reminds me of Dad. You know how he always seemed more interested in Rodney than in me—kind of like the men in the family stuck together. I always felt shut out of his world. And you give me those same disinterested feelings. But right now, you're making me think maybe you care a little more than I thought."

"I never knew you felt that way about your dad and your brother."

"I've thought about it a lot. And I really think it's true. In fact, I got hurt a lot in my family while I was growing up. No one really seemed to care that much about me. Maybe a lot of middle children feel that way. . . ."

With only a short break for dinner, Clarice and Bud talked for several hours about her past, their present inadequacies as husband and wife, and what should be done in the future. For the first time in her own adult life, Clarice began to face up to the fact that her family background, some of it long-forgotten, was contributing to her weight problem as well as to her obsession with Christian psychology.

"Clarice," Bud said before they went to bed. "It's really not that I dislike your weight so much; I just don't like to see you doing unhealthy things to yourself. Maybe I don't have a very good way of showing it. . . . Look, you may not believe this, coming from me, but I want to help. Maybe we can even pray about it or something. . . ?"

I can't believe he said that! I feel like I'm dreaming. How did he know?

That night, sleepless with excitement, Clarice reconsidered the evening's surprising turn of events. *Maybe Bud's not such a "carnal Christian" after all. I guess he's been tuned in to God in ways I haven't. Starting tomorrow, I'm going back on my diet. But then I'm going to see if God can help me get to the bottom of what's making me act this way. It's time I got well. . . .*

A *LOOK* INWARD—TAKING INVENTORY

It is at this point that we come to AA's "searching and fearless moral inventory"—a searching LOOK inward.

Ugh! you may say. On the surface, the thought of taking time to sort out your personal history may seem boring. Or too time-consuming. Or even excessively self-centered. Besides, why in the world would anyone want to feel hurtful feelings all over again?

Why? Because facing our difficulties is the way to overcome them permanently. Facing past and present pitfalls makes it possible for us to move ahead, unhindered, toward health.

The Personal Inventory on pages 131–34 is offered as a guide to help you LOOK inward as a step of uncovering any hidden emotions remaining from yesterday that are adversely affecting your behavior today. The test provides an avenue for effective self-therapy. But a word of caution: if you find the recounting of some past experience exceptionally or overwhelmingly painful, I strongly encourage you to seek professional help.

In taking inventory, you may learn some things you didn't expect to about yourself. One inventory taker painfully wrote,

> I began my inventory by making a list of all the things I hated in my father. I then took all the sentences dealing with his character defects, crossed out the word "he" and wrote in the word "I." It was quite a shock to see what was written there. At first, I just couldn't believe it . . .

If Clarice had known about the following test, it might have helped her to ask herself the right questions and to make the proper decisions about overcoming her addictive behavior. I think you'll find it very useful—I know I did!

As you make your journey through the questions, you'll find yourself being led through the jungles of almost-forgotten years. Here's fair warning: there are traps, snares, and quicksand in there. Avoid getting hung up on trying to analyze "why?" Don't play amateur "shrink" with yourself! Walk through at a healthy pace and don't sink into a mire of self-scrutiny. Perhaps setting a time limit will help you move ahead. And maybe praying the prayer of King David will assist you as you seek to be forthright and honest.

> Search me, O God, and know my heart;
> Try me and know my anxious thoughts;
> And see if there be any hurtful way in me,
> And lead me in the everlasting way.[1]

LOOK AT THE SOURCE OF YOUR PAIN

A large portion of your "fearless inventory" will involve facing past hurts in our lives.

Remember, a lot of us with obsessive personalities are the way we are because we are trying to desensitize ourselves to *pain*. Through the years, our souls (mind, emotions, and will) store up life experiences, including negative emotions such as fear, shame, and past rejections. If these emotions are not dealt with, they begin to rise up and spill over into our conscious minds. We then may find ourselves in a panic, choosing a behavior that will "cover up" the unwanted feelings. This is the way an addictive behavior can develop. When we "fix" our feelings by covering them up, the problem is buried. But it is buried alive, and it is almost sure to come back to haunt us:

> We search the world over for someone or something we can control that will take away this painful feeling of inadequacy and we will become strongly attached or even addicted to any person, substance, behavior or goal that promises to relieve or blot our pain and sense of alienation.[2]

---

1. Psalms 139:23–24.
2. J. Keith Miller, *Hope in the Fast Lane: A New Look at Faith in a Compulsive World* (San Francisco: Harper & Row, 1987), 51.

When pain from the past (or maybe even the present!) threatens, it seems much easier to become involved in compulsive behavior rather than to deal with the root cause of our appetites.

A good definition of compulsive behavior, in fact, could be "any behavior that will relieve the threat of pain or confrontation." Narcotics, remember, are called "painkillers," and private obsessions can be painkillers, too. We self-medicate ourselves with our fatal attractions.

If we're honest, we realize that we've got to get to the root of that pain in order to be healed. So that's one important point of LOOKing inward.

After all, life isn't supposed to be one continual offensive operation against pain. We're supposed to *feel* pain, of course—it's one of the body's protective mechanisms, a sign that we need to take some action. But we're not meant to live our lives on the defensive because of pain that has happened in the past. A person who is continually on the defensive never really experiences the joy of living now.

Much like our comic-strip friend Linus, some of us have been carrying around our addictive behaviors like security blankets, feeling warmed and relieved by them. We believe the lie that what we crave must be good for us and necessary to us because it brings relief and makes us happy. Yes, food brings relief, but too much or the wrong kinds of foods also clog our arteries, throw our body chemistry out of tilt, and make us fat. "His voice" answering the phone may bring a flood of relief—until he hangs up and we're left alone wondering who answered his phone first. . . .

Many of us compulsive types have a kind of "learned helplessness." We are unable to take independent action because we were taught to depend on others for happiness, to wait for it to arrive, or to have it "made" for us.

It's time we learned—the "happiness" ball is in our court.

We must learn, through looking honestly at ourselves, to stop avoiding, masking, or drowning out our pain. Pain is a signal that something is wrong! Running away from it got us into our addictions. LOOKing inward and allowing ourselves to "feel" our pain will help lead us out of it.

LOOK AT THE NEED FOR FORGIVENESS

Another part of your "fearless" inventory will involve facing the times you have hurt others. Are there people who have felt the pain, perhaps indirectly, of your addiction? Because of money spent? Because you just weren't there or were not giving your full attention? Maybe a relationship precious to you has suffered a crippling blow. You have the power to begin to undo your wrong choices by listing these in your inventory, asking forgiveness, and considering some ways you can make amends. The list may be small—just one or two names—but it is vital.

We've all got reason to be ashamed of items in our past: "If we say that we have no sin, we deceive ourselves, and the truth is not in us."[3] We're all in the same boat—the Sin Cruise Line—and it's taking us down the proverbial river. "Sin" is more than simply breaking the Ten Commandments (which, by the way, are not multiple choice). Sin is an attitude of independence from God, which can sometimes be an act of omission as well as commission.

In other words, sin isn't just what we do, it's also what we *don't* do. And if we do nothing about the accumulating guilt, it can cripple us. As Erma Bombeck says, "Guilt is the gift that keeps on giving . . ."

But there's more to that Scripture I just quoted: "If we confess our sins, [God] is faithful and just to forgive us our sins, and to cleanse us from all unrighteousness."[4] Listing our sins against others, asking forgiveness, and being willing to make amends will keep them from lingering under the surface as guilt, and further fueling our addictive tendencies.

Forgiveness is an absolutely vital part of recovering from obsessive behavior because it is key to the way God handles the messes we make of our lives and the world.

What do I mean? One of the first things we need to keep in mind about God is that *God loves us.* (Perhaps you weren't introduced to him as a loving God, but I urge you to accept

---

3. First John 1:8, KJV.
4. First John 1:1–9, KJV.

this fact about him anyway. It will become more real to you as you experience it in the recovery process.) And since we're not exactly perfect, and he is, there must be a reason why he's not always mad at us.

There is a reason. It's called forgiveness.

Forgiveness is God's way of releasing us from all our faults and mistakes and bad points. When we take a good LOOK at ourselves, confess what we've done, and ask forgiveness, God wipes our slates clean. He sets us free from our past guilt—free to step out into the future. But he does ask something from us. He wants us to do for others the same thing he's done for us.

God wants us to be forgiving, too.

LOOKing inward, then, also involves giving up our right to our feelings of revenge, bitterness, or anger toward people who have hurt us. People in the past may have been responsible for our problems *then,* but we're responsible for our problems *now.*

Doing our part of forgiving and letting go of the past does more than release us from our own guilt, however. It also helps bring old hurts and losses to the surface so we can mourn them and then release them. For instance, the act of conscious forgiveness may well cause you to reexperience a loss of love in your past. You may resent someone's lack of understanding, or their lack of response to your silent cry of need. But once you face this loss, you can grieve properly and then begin to heal.

Now is the time, then, to pray over your list of names, deliberately forgiving as well as blessing each name. In the book *Alcoholics Anonymous,* a person in recovery makes these observations:

> If you have a resentment you want to be free of, if you will pray for the person or the thing that you resent, you will be free. If you will ask in prayer for everything you want for yourself to be given to them, you will be free. Ask for their health, their prosperity, their happiness, and you will be free. Even when you don't really want it for them, and your prayers are only words, go ahead and do it

anyway. Do it everyday for two weeks and you will find you have come to mean it and to want it for them, and you will realize that where you used to feel bitterness and resentment and hatred, you now feel compassionate understanding and love.[5]

LOOK UP—TO GOD

So, having looked within, are you ready to allow God to remove your defects? When they are gone, what will be left? More space in which to *live,* for one thing!

```
Life is what happens to us
while we're worrying about
       something else!
```

Having looked honestly at your shortcomings, are you ready to ask God, humbly, to remove them? Humility comes naturally when you realize your need and recognize the fact that you don't "deserve" his help. You know you didn't "earn" his kindness. It is a gift—a humbling gift:

> God resists the proud, but gives grace to the humble. Therefore, submit to God. Resist the devil, and he will flee from you. Draw near to God, and he will draw near to you. Humble yourselves in the sight of the Lord and he will lift you up.[6]

It's time to LOOK, all right. LOOK *up!* Ask for God's forgiveness. Christ died so that you might be forgiven your sins for the asking. You don't have to continue to suffer for the things that have happened to you or even the things you've done wrong. Jesus died for that! He paid your price.

---

5. Quoted in Claire W., *"God, Help Me Stop"* (San Diego: Books West, 1982).

6. Author's paraphrase of 1 Peter 5:5–10, based on the KJV.

LOOK TO THE PRESENT AND THE FUTURE

Perhaps now you can understand why it is necessary to squarely face the past, eye to eye, and deal with it once and for all. Then we can leave the past behind and move into the future. The Bible speaks of "forgetting what lies behind and reaching forward to what lies ahead. . . ."[7] And those things that lie ahead can be ours, free from the crippling disabling power of past pain, with the help of another little tool.

LOOK TO FOLLOWING THROUGH

It's time to say it—be brave! Repeat after me the "D Word":

```
                      Discipline.
```

Discipline may not be your strong suit (as I've said, it's not mine), but we have to have at least a little of it if we want to get better. And looking at where "the D word" came from can help give us an idea of how to get it. *Discipline* is related to the word *disciple,* or follower. And that's where LOOKing to God will take us.

Specific disciplines, of course, have little value in themselves. But they are important because they put us in line with God so he can grant to us the freedom we seek. Discipline alone is not the answer; but discipline can help lead us to the answer!

With God's help, then, we're going to have the discipline to follow through on the process of cleaning up our act. We're going to get rid of whatever tempts us to backslide into addictive behavior. This may mean tossing out all the sweets in the house. Canceling our cable subscription. Finding new friends. Canceling a class we've signed up for. Getting too busy to pick up the phone. We're going to LOOK out for the temptations that "so easily beset us."

---

7. Philippians 3:13.

Perhaps most important, we're going to *follow through* on putting our forgiveness into action. One thing we *know* God has said—he's put it in writing enough times—is that we are to actively seek reconciliation with people we have hurt and those who have hurt us. Even after we've asked God's forgiveness for what we've done and forgiven those who have hurt us, we need to *follow through* on forgiveness by actually asking other people to forgive us or by making amends some other way.

"I'm sorry. I was wrong." Those little words gag many of us—we simply can't get them to come out of our mouths! But they are absolutely necessary if we are to deal with the past and move on. So how on earth do we go about asking forgiveness?

The best way to start out is by being honest, straightforward, and brief. There's no need to explain unpleasant behavior—explanations usually come out sounding like excuses, anyway. Face-to-face conversations are best, of course, better than phone calls (unless we can't afford the airfare!). Letters can be either eloquent or disastrous, depending upon our writing skills. Whatever the form we choose, we need to make amends in order to clear our consciences, to right the wrongs we've caused, and to mend broken relationships.

Are you willing to give it a try? Before facing the individual, why not try writing out what you want to say? This private "rehearsal" can be so helpful. It will give you opportunity to consider the different courses your conversation may take. And it will enable you to prepare for possible negative consequences such as:

- rejection,
- refusal to forgive,
- embarrassment,
- need to write a check (pay back),
- need to work overtime, or
- retaliation.

Uh-oh! I can almost see you throwing down the book in dismay. Why go through the agony of such a terrible ordeal?

Trust me! There really are two good reasons. First, because we're committed to healing, and we want to leave nothing behind us that may involve continuing grief or pain. But there is an even better reason than that. Christ taught us, even if we are not holding anything against someone else, that we should remember if someone "has something against" us.[8] If we know that there is unfinished business between ourselves and someone else (assuming the other person hasn't unreasonably rejected our efforts in the past), we are obliged to go and "be reconciled to" that person.

Think about it. What are you going to do—with your follow through?

Finally, while we're on the subject of discipline, here are a few practical suggestions for maintaining the discipline of happiness. Remember, the happiness ball is in your court! So bounce some of these around. Try setting aside a specific period of time—say ten days—to work these disciplines into your life:

1. Plan your day ahead.
2. Become productive at meaningful work.
3. Feel your feelings.
4. Express your feelings to a friend.
5. Consciously set worrying aside.
6. Seek meaningful friendships.
7. Lower your unrealistic expectations, but don't give up hope!
8. Develop a more positive outlook.
9. Forgive yourself and others.
10. Develop your spiritual side.

And, while you're at it, you just may want to pray this familiar, unforgettable prayer—a prayer that has helped generations of addicts—as you move ahead with your new life:

> **God grant me the serenity**
> **to accept the things I cannot change,**
> **the courage to change the things I can,**
> **and the wisdom to know the difference.**

---

8. Matthew 5:23.

my personal inventory
a tool for looking into your life

In order to change your present behavior, you need to release the hold your hurtful past experiences have on you today. Walking through this Personal Inventory will help you let go of the past, grab on to the present, and get ready for the future:

1. Using the following grid as a guide, review the hurtful experiences of your past which you feel could be affecting your behavior today. Include the age you were when you had the experience, name the person(s) who have hurt you, and describe the hurtful experience and the effect of the experience on you (your thoughts, feelings, and behavior—attitude, word, and deed). Be honest, be thorough, and be specific, but don't get bogged down! This inventory is intended to help dig you out, not bury you!

HOW I HAVE BEEN HURT

Age	Hurt by	Incident	Effect on Me
Child (0–12)			
Adoles. (13–18)			
Adult (18–)			

2. Now that you have looked into your own hurts, it's time
    to make a similar list of the hurts you may have caused
    others. Be brave; dealing with guilt is just as important
    as dealing with other forms of pain.

HOW I HAVE HURT OTHERS

Age	Person I Hurt	Incident	Effect on Person I Hurt
Child (0–12)			
Adoles. (13–18)			
Adult (18–)			

3. Having listed past pain and guilt, you can now begin to
    let go of them. Go down your list and consciously
    release each hurtful experience—"change your mind"
    about it. For each experience where you have been hurt
    by another person(s), say aloud, "I will no longer blame
    _____ and the time they _____.
    I will not use this hurt as an excuse for my behavior.

4. To be completely free from past hurtful experiences,
    you must forgive—pardon the persons who hurt you
    and yourself as well. This forgiveness is essential to
    your healing. Forgiveness begins with an act of your
    will: I choose to forgive _____
    for _____.

5. Although we are not in a position to "forgive" God, we
    do need to "let go" of our tendency to blame him for our

hurtful experiences. We can't afford to be angry and resentful toward him or to think he either "caused" them or "failed to intervene" on our behalf. Go down your list and pray out loud about each hurtful experience, expressing to God that you don't blame him for whatever transpired and that you believe Romans 8:28—"All things work together for good to them that love God, to them who are the called according to his purpose" (KJV).

6. You are now free to grab on to the present, to reform— "set right" or "make straight"—your life. Having repented and forgiven, go down your list again and see if there is anything you can to help yourself become healthier or to make amends where your past hurt has caused you to hurt someone else. Write down your plans in the following chart:

WHAT CAN I DO

To Help Heal (Where others have hurt me)	To Help Make Amends (Where I've hurt others)

7. Now that you have grabbed on to everything you can do (your part) and expressed your determination to do it, grab onto everything God has done for you (his part) and express your dependence upon him. To release the hold of your past experiences and change your present

behavior, you must work in partnership with God. List
the things you would like him to do to restore you in
regard to past hurts (remaining open to the fact that he
might have some strategies you haven't thought of yet).

```
┌──────────────────────────────────────────────────┐
│               WHAT GOD CAN DO . . .                │
│                                                    │
│                                                    │
│                                                    │
│                                                    │
│                                                    │
│                                                    │
│                                                    │
│                                                    │
│                                                    │
│                                                    │
└──────────────────────────────────────────────────┘
```

8. Even though you have finished your inventory, you are
   still human. You will always have weaknesses that
   cause feelings and emotions leading to negative behavior. That's the bad news. But the good news is God
   forgives your obsessions and your negative behavior,
   and he is eager to help you deal with your weaknesses.
   With that in mind, learn this procedure and repeat it
   often:

   • Confess to God your negative behavior and the character
     weaknesses that cause it.
   • Ask him to help you *release the past*—letting go of your
     hurtful experiences.
   • Ask him to help you *reform the present*—to grab onto
     repentance and forgiveness and to depend upon him.
   • Ask him to *restore the future*—helping you become the
     person you really are and enabling you to move forward.

7

listen!

three stages of breaking free

The recovery process we've begun with STOP and LOOK is never supposed to come to an end. Recovery from private obsessions is ongoing; it's a process, not an event. But now that we've completed our personal inventory, instead of looking behind us all the time, let's begin to deal with some present realities that are coming toward us.

And that brings us to the third step in our break-free strategy: LISTEN.

The LISTEN step involves three stages. We begin by listening to our own feelings.

Next, we allow others to hear our dilemma, and we listen to what they may have to say.

Finally, we seek to listen to the voice of God. Once we sit at his feet with open hearts, and seek his counsel through his Son Jesus, our Heavenly Father's love and inspiration will be poured out upon us. His wisdom and guidance will fill our minds with hope and peace.

But listening, as most of us know, isn't easy. Most of us enjoy conversations immensely—usually because we are the ones doing all the talking! Worse yet, if we are bad about listening to people, we can be absolutely hopeless when it comes to listening to God. His "still, small voice" seldom breaks through the noisy interference that surrounds our lives. And sometimes, especially if we're unaware of how much he loves us, we're almost afraid to hear what he might have to say anyway.

For that reason, the LISTEN is more than the final step of recovery. LISTENing is a lifelong quest.

LISTEN TO YOUR FEELINGS

So. Are you really ready to make a clean slate of the past? I hope so! And if your answer is yes, let's move on the first area of "listening." Recovering from addiction means listening to what our own hearts are telling us. It's time we developed the fine art of "feeling our feelings"—instead of covering them up with all kinds of frantic activity.

Many of us have an unhealthy habit of withdrawing emotionally to avoid feeling pain. Isn't it time we not only faced our feelings, and confessed them to ourselves, but also ran the risk of being vulnerable? If we accept the fact that our feelings are neither right nor wrong, we enable ourselves to examine them without guilt.

Why do we imagine that we can live our lives without feelings? "I'd like to make a motion that we face reality," Bob Newhart once said on one of his TV shows. Let's do that! If we get in the habit of STOPPING and LOOKING when we sense an unwanted feeling rising up and then learn to LISTEN to ourselves to examine what's happening, we can shed light on our true feelings and determine their "normal" size.

"Down" emotions, for example, are natural; it's not normal to feel only good feelings. Tell yourself that it's OK sometimes to feel:

- rejected,
- intimidated,
- angry,
- disappointed,
- hungry, or
- depressed.

All these are involuntary emotional responses. They need not be covered up or hidden. At times I say out loud to myself something like, "Lee, you feel disillusioned now," or "Lee, you're really disappointed, aren't you?" Once I understand my negative feelings and label them, I'm far more able to cope with them.

Much like mushrooms, some of our bad feelings swell in the "dark"—when we don't know what's causing them. Just as physical pain tells us that something is wrong with our bodies, unpleasant emotional feelings tell us something is out of place in our lives. By dulling either pain, we may allow a minor situation to become overwhelming.

NOT REPRESS AND SUPPRESS; CONFESS AND EXPRESS

Expressing these feelings—both positive and negative—to ourselves will decrease our obsessive submerging of them. Speak it out loud:

- "I'm really furious! I've never been more angry!"
- "Oh-oh, I feel intimidated again. . . . "
- "If I were honest, I'd have to say I'm really lonely right at the moment."
- "I don't want to feel hurt, but my heart is aching so badly."

These thoughts help place labels on our surging emotions. We are "owning" our own negative feelings—taking possession of them. That's "legal," and not a cause for guilt. How we deal with what we feel makes all the difference in the world.

But the fact that our negative emotions are natural doesn't mean they are acceptable excuses for negative behavior— including private obsessions. The Bible says, for example, that we are to "be angry, and yet do not sin"[1]—thus allowing for the natural emotion of anger if not for the outbursts that sometimes accompany it. So it is with other emotions—don't pretend they don't exist, but don't let them lead you astray, either.

---

1. Ephesians 4:26.

And, by the way, if the blues are haunting us, let's not take the songwriter's advice anymore: "I've got to have fun, fun, fun to keep the blues on the run." Blues, blahs, black rages, whatever—we've given up covering up with "fun," busy, or otherwise anesthetizing activities.

In other words, whatever the emotion you're dealing with, keep short accounts. And don't reach for your "fix" behavior. Take an on-the-spot inventory. Admit your wrong part in the situation and communicate your feelings to yourself and to God. Let the people involved know who you are, what you think, what you feel, and what you need. Then move forward.

LISTEN TO LOVE

But listening to yourself doesn't just mean dealing with your negative feelings. So often, the pain people bear comes from their unawareness of being loved, either by God or man. An important part of LISTENing, therefore, is to remember those who really care about you and thank God for them. Try to grasp God's love for you by faith, while asking him to demonstrate it to you through other people. Think of all this as counting your "love blessings" (instead of sheep!).

And when you put your head on your pillow at night, do a "bed check" of the day as well. Thank God for all the positive things you can think of in your life. Then LISTEN to see if you've left any unfinished business. When used in such as way, LISTENing becomes a tool of ongoing recovery.

LISTEN TO ANOTHER PERSON

It's important be aware that recovery from compulsions is not really an event; it is a process. And it's not something we should try to accomplish with God's help alone; we need to share our struggle to someone else. And by the way, the AA Twelve Steps specify "another human being." Confessing to your dog won't cut it!

Drawing another person into the picture is truly the most courageous step of all! When you do that, you are faced with real accountability. You're not *excusing* yourself anymore. You are no longer simply a "prisoner of circumstance."

Up until now, guilt and pain have been your chosen wardens and your prison has been locked from the inside. Making that "fearless moral inventory" of yourself enabled you to find the key. Now, confessing to another person will unlock the door!

The listening ear of another person helps us gain release from our obsessions. We must not only listen to the voice of the Spirit of God, but to ourselves. And then we must make ourselves vulnerable enough to listen to the advice and counsel of a chosen mentor, a trusted friend. Recovery is more solidly and soundly experienced within the context of healthy relationships. Proverbs 28:13 makes this clear: "He who conceals his transgressions will not prosper, but he who confesses and forsakes them will find compassion."

> **Recovery seldom happens**
> **in a vacuum.**

SARAH

Do you remember Sarah, the older woman we met earlier? She was obsessed with housework and church activities. And, if you recall, she had become exceptionally annoyed with her church's secretary over an unclear announcement in the church bulletin. But when she went in to take the young woman to task, something amazing happened. To Sarah's amazement, that incident led to an unexpected friendship which developed gradually and quietly over a period of several weeks—and which made the difference in helping Sarah get over her private obsessions.

Jeannie, the church secretary, was a gentle young woman of thirty-five who felt a deep sense of concern for Sarah. When first confronted by the older woman, she apologized profusely for her error. Then she managed to talk Sarah into going to lunch with her. They went out once, then again and again.

It wasn't long before Sarah was actually confiding in Jeannie, who could quickly see how very lonely the widow was. More important, as Sarah talked, she began to get some insight into why her life was the way it was. She could see that all her busyness and efficiency were simply ways to mask the emptiness of her solitary lifestyle.

With sensitive insight, Jeannie began to help Sarah see that her delicious baking was offered to the church as a sort of "please love me" sacrifice, and her overly clean house was a way of proving her value as a person. Sarah knew she still missed her deceased husband terribly and was struggling with a sense of abandonment. But now, for the first time, she could see how her pain was causing her to cut people off.

Jeannie and her husband began to invite Sarah to their home and to visit hers. Before long she was sharing Sunday dinners and holidays with them.

And then Sarah did a very difficult thing. In one of her talks with Jeannie, she told this trusted friend that she was aware of her compulsive behavior. She asked for Jeannie's help with overcoming her irritable ways when dealing with interruptions and unplanned visitors. The two friends agreed that Sarah's policy must always be, "people come first."

"God, give me patience," she murmured tearfully one day as Jeannie held her hand. "Have I been abrupt with anyone? Have I been overly concerned about unimportant matters? Please help me, God, to feel your love, and to show it to others."

"And Lord," Jeannie prayed, squeezing Sarah's hand, "Help this dear lady to know how very precious she is to you, and to me, too. Bless her, Lord, with a sense of your delight in her."

LOCATING A *LISTEN* ING EAR

How do you find another person to confide in? I would guess that you'll discover some suitable person readily at hand. Ask God to confirm who this confidant is for you. It may be a member of the clergy, or maybe a counselor, or even a trusted friend. If you are "only as sick as your secrets," then you're going to get well soon! The role of this good friend is to be a hearing ear, a nonjudgmental shoulder to lean on. He or she will agree with you that a problem exists, and will be glad to stand beside you in seeing you through.

> **Confess your faults**
> **one to another,**
> **And pray for one another,**
> **that you may be healed.** [2]

You have admitted your faults to God. You've entrusted them to another person. Now, like the proverbial "new broom that sweeps clean," you've opened up the lines of communication. And now you can receive insights and information that will enhance your commitment, encourage your accountability, and ensure your ultimate freedom.

LISTEN FOR TRUTH

You may recall that we said the STOP step of recovery is for the body. It involves calling a halt to unwholesome activity and making a new start with God.

The LOOK step benefits the soul. It involves "cleaning house" by means of a personal inventory.

LISTEN is for the spirit, an area which needs to be open and pure before God. Spiritual health requires truthfulness "in the inner parts," as David the psalmist once said.[3] That's why when you decide to confide in a caring individual, you should be specific, not indirect. Here's the way your side of the conversation might go:

> "I'm having a problem, and need your listening ear."
> "I am struggling with _____."
> "_____ has become addictive to me."
> "It may seem small to you, but it matters to me."
> "I've confessed to God that I'm powerless over this
>   behavior. I want to confess to you; it's humbling. . . ."

---

2. James 5:16, adapted from the KVJ.
3. Psalms 51:6, NIV.

"The desire hits me most when _____."
"I normally respond by _____."
"I am seeking God's help; I want to change."

Yes, you will want to swallow hard before you begin. After all, your confidante may not have a clue about your problem! No doubt you'll be tempted to think, "She'll be shocked and lose all her respect for me!" If you've chosen your friend carefully, that's not likely. True friends respect us far more when we are honest, forthright, and courageous.

And, by the way, don't hesitate to confess to another because you're afraid you'll embarrass yourself with "repeat behavior." In other words, don't expect to be "cured" before you confide. "Relapsing" can be expected as part of the recovery process. And having a friend involved can pull you out of a relapse that much faster:

> Two are better than one because they have a good return for their labor. For if either of them falls, the one will lift up his companion. But woe to the one who falls when there is not another to lift him up.[4]

A *LISTEN*ING PARTNERSHIP

No matter what the private obsession involved, I have found that signing an agreement with your "partner" solidifies a commitment and assists accountability. (Such an agreement may tie you together in friendship for an extended period of time.) On the following page you will find an idea for such a "contract." Use it, or make up your own version.

Well, there you have it! You have given your friend permission to check on your progress. Your confidant has committed herself/himself to your recovery process. By now you should have breathed a deep sigh of relief! You have authorized someone else to "meddle" in your affairs, to "keep an eye on you."

---

4. Ecclesiastes 4:9–10.

CONFIDANT'S AGREEMENT

My friend, _____ , has chosen me as a confidant, and I have heard the confession of wrongs as to her "private obsessions." She has revealed her true self to me, and acknowledged the exact nature of her problem. She has identified and pinpointed her private obsession(s) as _____. She has a sincere desire to STOP, and been courageous enough to LOOK inwardly in review of her Personal Inventory. She has entrusted me with her confession, and is beginning to LISTEN.

I will keep all that is said with regard to this matter in strict confidence.

I agree with my friend that she has a problem over which she is presently powerless. She has expressed a desire to change, and I believe she is willing to do what it takes to bring about that change. I commit myself, in prayer and in whatever personal support I can provide, to her recovery process.

For the next thirty days I will attempt to keep in daily contact, be a listening ear, and risk asking hard questions. To the best of my ability (insofar as I am able) I will not allow my friend to excuse her behavior or enable her to continue it. I will listen to her, and will assist her in learning to listen to the voice of her own conscience.

I recognize, along with my friend, that total recovery is only possible by believing in the work of Christ and living in total dependence upon God.

_____ / _____   _____ / _____
Confidant's Signature   Date   Confider's Signature   Date

Perhaps you'll want to discuss some time-line goals or challenges, such as:

- I refuse to watch TV for one week.
- I commit not to call _____ for forty-eight hours.
- I will confide in my friend when the "binge again" pangs hit.
- I will refuse to work this next weekend.

Make your challenges and goals bite-sized so you will not grow discouraged, so you can see that God is working on your behalf.

*LISTEN*ING GROUPS: UNITE AND CONQUER!

Either America is crazy for support groups, or support groups keep America from going crazy. The front of *Newsweek* magazine[5] reports "Support Groups Are the Answer for 15 Million Americans." Anyone who suffers from a private obsession (except possibly an addiction to support groups!) can benefit from such a LISTENing aid.

A truly beneficial group would be one which simply sees itself as a means to an end—individual freedom—not one that becomes a crutch or a substitute for growth. View it simply as a temporary support until you get your own footing in freedom.

To begin with, your "support group" can consist of just your confidant and yourself to start. But if, through your own honest confession to others, you discover someone else struggling with the same problem you have, why not invite him or her to join in the discussion? Although "Pack Rats Anonymous" or "Telephone Junkies Anonymous" may not be as desperate as "Alcoholics Anonymous," sharing can be mutually beneficial when it comes to seeking answers and receiving motivation.

Why not form a small group of understanding people who are willing to talk about their private struggles? Or you may find that such a group (such as Overeaters Anonymous) already exists in your community. As in AA or similar recovery groups, you will join together on the common ground that you are "powerless" and are working toward complete freedom.

I can't help but wonder if Christ might not feel more comfortable in an "Anonymous" meeting than in many of our church gatherings. The weakness of many small groups in churches is the Pharisaic spirit that whispers, "I thank Thee that I am not like these others. . . ." We're far better off admitting that we're all in a same boat called "Fellow Strugglers." In an "we've all failed" atmosphere, anyone can freely confess "I need more help. I can't make it"—and in confessing, gain the strength they need.

---

5. 5 February 1990.

LISTEN TO THE HIGHER POWER

Our LISTEN step wouldn't be complete without including God's voice as well. How do we hear him? No, you don't have to be a mystic with glassy eyes to receive a heavenly transmission. The "channel" for hearing from God was opened by Christ on the cross; no more sacrifice is necessary.

To listen to God, read his words in the Bible. Tell him how you really feel. Then sit quietly and wait for the encouragement and guidance of his "still, small voice."

The Bible is God's love letter to you. Do you have an easy-to-read version of it? If you're new to the Bible, don't try to decipher one with all those "thees and thous"; find a plain-talking version. The new edition called *The Book* is available in most bookstores. If you have been reading one particular version of the Bible for awhile, why not treat yourself to a brand new translation or an updated paraphrase? You'll find it gives a refreshing perspective to those timeless truths.

Joining a group of fellow believers who honestly want to change will also help you learn to LISTEN to God.

"There are too many hypocrites in your church," one man snapped to his friend.

The friend replied, "Well, then, why not join us? You'll feel right at home!"

No, the church is not made up of perfect people. It's a good thing it isn't—that way, we all qualify! (I know this is true; my car was recently rear-ended by another car bearing the bumper sticker: "Christians aren't perfect, just forgiven.")

We all need to make conscious contact with God through prayer. Ask for his will to be done in your earthly body, just as his will is done in heaven. Ask for the power of his Spirit to carry out what he desires in your life. And then relax. Through the ongoing strategy of STOP, LOOK, and LISTEN, he will help you move steadily toward a happier, healthier, more meaningful life.

LISTEN TO FIND MOTIVATION FOR THE JOURNEY

Listening is an upward step—toward heaven. But is that enough motivation to keep us on the often-difficult path of recovery? "Who cares about 'pie in the sky, bye and bye,' anyway?" you may say (or think, subconsciously). "I want my slice *now!*"

The good news is we *don't* have to wait till heaven to get a taste of it right here on earth. And the STOP! LOOK! LISTEN! steps I have outlined are precisely the way for us to experience that earthly sampling of heaven. I call it RPJ—as you will see in the next chapter— and it's one of the most potent motivators around.

8

---

the power
of rpj

finding the motivation to keep on

Are you beginning to get the picture? Our private obsessions are really nothing more than a mad scramble to hide ourselves from impending or perceived unpleasantness—pain, boredom, anxiety, intimidation, guilt. But the problem is, we can't keep running, hiding, or covering up what we must inevitably face. We can't keep trying desperately to save ourselves from uneasy sensations. If we seek to save our lives, we will lose them, buried under another pile of compulsive cover-ups. So let's refuse to crawl under our security blankets—

- digging into our piles of pack-rat junk,
- hiding behind the cover of yet another good book,
- submerging ourselves in a career,
- warming ourselves with constant thoughts of "him," or
- pursuing whatever else our personal obsession may be.

Here's the bottom line: the temporary good must be sacrificed for the ultimate good. We know, ultimately, that the best thing available to us is inner peace, and that peace will cost us a compulsion or two. Rest assured, however, that the sense of peace will last far longer than the temporary buzz provided by our addiction of choice.

Why, then, do we persist in our private obsessions? No one—not even the most spiritual—seems immune to them. Can a Christian father still be a sportsaholic and neglect his kids because of his private obsession? Can a Christian woman be controlled by soap-opera schedules and hooked on romance novels and still be a sincere Christian wife? Can a sex addict be a Christian—or even a preacher?

The answer to all those questions, believe it or not, is a resounding "YES!"

After all, being Christian does not exempt us from being human—and that means that Christians are just as susceptible to human foibles as nonbelievers. If a man with the flu goes to a church service and receives Christ there, he is now a Christian man with the flu. Similarly, if a woman with a secret addiction to, say, utter cleanliness receives Christ, she is now a secretly addicted Christian woman, although she now has a resident Power to overcome her compulsive behavior. And long after they become Christians, both will be susceptible to developing either the flu or a secret addiction again.

Have you noticed how many preachers and religious leaders are making headlines these days? It's quite clear, with a couple of notable exceptions, that their fame has not come as a result of their "conscious contact with God." Whatever relationship they may have with the Lord, it evidently has not made them holy. And yet they persistently claim to know and believe in salvation through Jesus Christ.

Let's be honest. The spectrum of addiction has penetrated every segment of society, from the drug-addict street people to the porn-addict pulpit people. I know these things "ought not to be," but unfortunately, they exist. Sin and addiction know no boundaries; they cross all lines. No one is exempt!

If just being a Christian is not enough to keep us free from private obsessions, where can we find the motivation to change our questionable habits and persist in our recovery efforts? Much as we want to do "the right thing," I'm convinced we won't find that motivation until we're convinced of two things:

- that hidden obsessions are harmful, negative factors in our lives; and
- that something valuable will be lost if we don't get rid of them.

The first one's relatively easy. We've already determined that the "private obsessions" we've been talking about are draining us, driving us, and diverting us from healthy, happy living.

But the second point is equally important. To keep our motivation up, we must realize that, unless we reform, we're going to lose something we are not willing to live without. This chapter will help identify what will be lost—forfeited— in exchange for our addictions. We'll be able to determine whether or not a private obsession is worth the hidden price tag it bears. Have we counted the cost—really?

HOW DO I STAY MOTIVATED?

"So what if I have a little nagging habit that bugs me now and then. It's no big deal."

"My overindulgence is an occasional problem. I'm not really 'suffering' from it."

"If I am assured of heaven by faith in Christ, why clean up my act?"

Those are fair questions. It's not as if those of us with private obsessions are a danger to society! Our little hangup may not seem all that threatening or harmful—and after all, nobody's perfect. Besides, breaking bad habits is hard. So why put ourselves through all that?

Why bother to chase away all our "little foxes?"

Because, as the Bible says, they "spoil the vines!"[1]

It's not a question of perfection, but of our quality of life. God is not a Cosmic Killjoy. He wants us to enjoy our lives to their fullest. But in order for us to find freedom from hindrances, distractions, and guilt, we have to find some sort of ongoing inner motivation.

---

1. Song of Solomon 2:15.

Suppose I'm a few pounds overweight and, by the time Christmas is past, I've added another five pounds. On New Year's Day, I fully and enthusiastically commit to a new diet. But by the time the end of January rolls around, I'm no longer talking about dieting. I'm avoiding the bathroom scale and the full-length mirror. And I'm making all kinds of excuses for myself. The truth of the matter is, I simply "didn't care enough" to stick with it!

No matter what we're trying to accomplish, although others may provide encouragement, motivation has to emanate from inside us. So the question becomes, how do we find the motivation we need to keep fighting our private obsessions?

HEAVENLY MOTIVATION?

In many Christian circles, the classic motivator for "right behavior" has been the hope of heaven and the fear of hell. We are encouraged to act in a certain way because we are told that certain behavior will affect our "ultimate destination" or our standing with God.

Well, it's a debatable point, I'll admit, and I'm no theologian. But here's the way I've come to view the subject. The Bible believer can boast of being saved by faith—by the grace of God and not by his or her own works.[2] And so yes, we can still go to heaven in spite of our sins. We believe and trust that Christ paid the price for our sins and mistakes when he died on the cross. We don't have to cover the cost.

And no one who believes the Bible can, in good conscience, say that he is "doing his best to get to heaven." Heaven is God's gift to us, which we receive in exchange for our faith. It has nothing to do with our subsequent behavior. Those whose lives are "hidden with Christ in God," by faith, are assured that heaven is our destiny, not a destination we have to work to reach. If you have been reborn in the spirit, into the family of God, hell is not the place for you! God's spirit, dwelling in your body, would not be welcome there.

And so, I conclude,

---

2. Ephesians 2:8–9.

> **We cannot in good conscience**
> **_bribe_ people with heaven,**
> **and _blackmail_ them with hell.**

If God's goal were simply to get us to heaven, he might as well send along an instant heart attack to each one who receives Christ: Voila—eternal security!

But here's another way of looking at it:

> **God is not trying to get us to heaven;**
> **God is trying to get heaven _in_ us!**

Perhaps you grew up hearing the question, "Where will you be when the Lord returns?" That's known as "second coming" or "rapture" motivation. Will you be at the local bar? In Las Vegas? At the local porno theater watching an X-rated movie?

OK, it's true; he may return today. But that news is not supposed to be a threat; it is supposed to something to look forward to. Besides, he knows where you are and what you're doing whether he shows up in person or not!

A BETTER REASON: THE PROMISE OF THE KINGDOM

So if heaven is assured, and if God is watching anyway, where is the inspiration for unobsessed, addiction-free living? I'd like to offer you this life-changing motivation: *Breaking free of your private obsession will help bring you closer to the kingdom of God.*

Christ advised us to "seek first" this kingdom.[3] But what is it—really? Let's find out. And let's see how we can qualify for experiencing this "kingdom" right where we are now, here on earth. In doing so, I think we'll find sufficient incentive for overcoming all those faults and sins "that so easily beset us."

The meaning of the phrase "kingdom of God" implies *a condition* (state of being), as well as *a place* (destination). The

---

3. Matthew 6:33, NKJV.

literal Greek meaning of the phrase "kingdom of God" is
"reign of God," which implies a condition. The early Jewish
Christians had a traditional reluctance to speak the name of
God out loud; they considered it too sacred to be spoken. So
they often used the phrase "the kingdom of heaven" instead of
"kingdom of God." And hence, the connotation of the place—
heaven—began to take precedence over the original connotation of a condition—the reign of God.

I think those of us who are Christians can testify to the fact
that when we were born into the kingdom of God we didn't
wake up in a spiritual fantasyland. But if the kingdom is not a
place, what is it?

The apostle Paul defines the kingdom in these words:

> "The kingdom of God is not
> meat and drink [things]; but
> righteousness, and peace, and joy
> [a condition]." [4]

Anyone, in other words, can have an eternal relationship
with God (salvation) by simply receiving Christ's sacrifice for
sin. But only those who *clean up their act* qualify for his
reward (the kingdom). And only those who "keep [Jesus']
commandments"[5] experience the thrill of having genuine
righteousness(R), real peace(P), and overflowing joy(J)—I
call it my R-P-J.

And so . . . can a Christian woman live with her boyfriend?
Yes. But she can't have RPJ.

Can a Christian lie and cheat? Yes. But he can't experience
RPJ.

Could a preacher toy with homosexuality? Yes. But he
can't enjoy RPJ.

It's perfectly possible to have salvation without experiencing kingdom benefits.

---

4. Romans 14:17, KJV.
5. John 14:15.

DON'T GIVE UP YOUR INHERITANCE

A relationship with God can be instantly established by anyone who will trust Christ as Savior. It bears repeating: The work of Christ on the Cross is what "pays" for our sins, and our relationship with God is established independently from our actions. Our salvation is made certain by the "new birth" which follows our confession of faith in Christ; when we trust him, we are reborn into God's family. And when that happens, we are assured of heaven. Why would God send a child of his to hell?

And yet . . .

You realize it is possible to be a valid member of a rich family and still not get your inheritance, right? Although we may be legally adopted by God and thus have a legal relationship to him, his close friendship and his personal, priceless blessings—his fellowship—come to us on a different basis. We are talking about *relationship versus fellowship.* Through *obedience* we qualify for our "inheritance" in this wealthy family. When we live our lives God's way, we receive the matchless heritage of "kingdom living" right now.

The Bible specifically lists some forms of behavior which prevent believers from inheriting the kingdom of God. They include[6]:

fraud (cheating)	fornication
idolatry	adultery
effeminacy (homosexuality)	thef
coveting	drunkenness
reviling	extortion
uncleanness or filthiness	lasciviousness (loose living)
witchcraft (occult practices)	foolish (undisciplined) talk
variance (contention or dissension)	emulations (rivalry or competition)
wrath (strong anger)	strife
sedition (rebellion)	heresy
envy	murder
lust (illicit or excessive desire)	revelry
hatred	

6. Taken from 1 Corinthians 6:6–10 and Galatians 5:19–21.

Now, take a close look at the actions outlined on this list. If these actions prevent people from inheriting the kingdom, could "kingdom" possibly mean "heaven?" Can it be that anyone who gives in to "envyings" or "coveting" cannot go to heaven? Anyone who has experienced strong anger? Anyone who has had an extramarital affair? Anyone who has stirred up trouble? Any one who has told a dirty joke? It can't be true—none of us would ever make it!

No, we're not talking about salvation here; we're talking about inheritance. The Scripture makes it quite clear that if we participate in these things we will not receive the righteousness, peace and joy which is our heritage in Christ. Yes, we'll still get to heaven . . . but we may find ourselves miserable along the way! I view this withholding of "RPJ" as God's ace-in-the-hole in disciplining his children.

"But Lee," you cry out, "Shopping isn't on the list! Neither is overeating. Or being a pack rat. Or loving a man too much!"

It's true. Many of our "little foxes" aren't even mentioned. And yet you know, as well as I, that they, too, can get in the way of a fulfilling, gratifying life.

The problem with private obsessions, whether or not they are listed in the Bible as "no-nos," is that they have a powerful hold on us, and that control causes us to seek *them* first, not the kingdom. That is why:

The primary thing

is to keep the primary thing

as the primary thing!

We want to keep matters in their proper perspective. "Seek first the kingdom"—*that* is the primary thing! And when we do that, even at the price of a cherished private obsession, it is our heavenly Father's "good pleasure" to give us the kingdom![7]

---

7. Luke 12:32.

LEE AND RPJ

A music lover from way back, I long ago began to use music as a way of avoiding my problems. As a teenager, although I played first violin in many orchestras, I still had to escape my feeling of being "second fiddle" to everyone else. The study of drama and music filled my hours with song. Music was in my blood; the beat seemed to go on almost continuously in my head. I filled every moment with radio melodies and continual "background" music. Hardly an hour passed when I wasn't somehow surrounded by music— classical, pop, or praise.

My private obsession with TV began when my extensive traveling schedule did. I spoke across the country, and I found it was nice to have "someone" in the hotel rooms with me during my stay.

Because of these two "harmless" habits, there were very few quiet moments in which I could hear the "still, small voice" of the Spirit of God. Furthermore, my addiction to noise kept me from facing any necessary confrontations with myself.

The righteousness, peace, and joy which I sought was frequently drowned out by the continual distraction of a ceaseless din. Once I realized what I was doing, I decided it was time for a major change. During my STOP step, I "fasted" background noise—cut it off entirely. And I discovered a whole new world!

There was peace around, but I'd never heard it before. And in the silence, I discovered a new joy in communicating with God. I wasn't just talking to him; he was talking to me—and I could hear him!

What price did I pay? I had to take steps to (1) STOP the clamor, (2) LOOK into the roots of where and why the habit began, and (3) LISTEN to what the Lord was trying to transmit to me (while I was on a different wavelength). As a result of taking those steps, I am now more fully enjoying God's great treasure of righteousness, peace, and joy.

MOVE OVER, ESAU!

The Bible records both in Genesis 25:33 and in Hebrews 12:16 the story of how Esau sold his inheritance—his birthright—for an insignificant bowl of stew. It seems absurd to us in retrospect, but don't we do the same sort of thing at times?

Picture yourself with both hands full, weighing two choices. In one hand you hold the experience of righteousness, peace, and joy—RPJ. In the other lies the behavior you're going to trade for this "pearl of great price." [8] What is it? Another academic degree? Another shopping spree or mystery novel? Or perhaps (as the Bible list indicates), you are bartering RPJ for a little envy . . . rage . . . gossip. Now count the cost. Is your private obsession worth the cost? Really?

Move over, Esau . . . here we come.

Perhaps you realize you've sold your soul (the righteousness, peace, and joy in your soul) for your private obsession. Did you buy a pair of shoes you didn't really need? Your RPJ will cost you a return trip to the mall. Have you sold your inheritance to become a "Type-A" workaholic? Being restored will cost you time away from the job.

Figure 4 — Weighing Your Options

---

8. Matthew 13:4–6, KJV.

A person who is privately obsessed with church, or house cleaning, or Fido, or Kent 100s® may not be committing some big "sin." But their idolatry—putting anything above constant obedience to God—may well be depriving them of kingdom living. For them, the cost of experiencing RPJ will be giving up their private obsession.

In his excellent book, *Celebration of Discipline,* Richard Foster encourages us:

> Reject anything that is producing an addiction in you. TV? By all means sell your set or give it away. Any of the media that you cannot do without get rid of; radios, stereo, magazines, movies, newspapers, books, tapes. Rid yourself of anything that has a grip on your heart; refuse to be a slave to anything but God.[9]

The New Testament does not clearly spell out a giant list of "thou shalt nots." As a matter of fact, the apostle Paul says, "I know and am convinced in the Lord Jesus that *nothing* is unclean in itself."[10] And yet he adds: "All things are lawful for me, but not all things are profitable. All things are lawful for me, but I will not be *mastered* by anything."[11]

```
Good is the enemy
of the best!
```

As God's children, we are free to enjoy music, watch TV, work hard, occasionally pig out, enjoy close relationships, go for therapy—all of these. But when they become IT, that poor substitute for tranquility and satisfaction (RPJ), we've blown it! We've become slaves to our own activities.

It is because our private obsessions invariably rule us—our time, our social life, our finances, our attitudes, our spiritual

---

9. Richard Foster, *Celebration of Discipline* (San Francisco: Harper & Row, 1978), 79.

10. Romans 14:14, emphasis added.

11. 1 Corinthians 6:12, emphasis added.

life—that we must break free of them. And our reward for
breaking free will be—we are promised—the wonderful
experience of RPJ.

A FRAGILE FREEDOM

Romans 14:14 clearly instructs us that there may not be
anything wrong (unclean) with certain activities, but it also
warns: "To him who thinks anything to be unclean, to him it
is unclean [wrong]."[12] In other words, some choices depend
on individual circumstances. There is nothing inherently
wrong with eating a dessert. But before I reach for my
mother-in-law's fabulous strawberry cake (eight hundred
calories a slice), I must inquire within myself: "Yes or no?" If
my conscience is clear, I can then enjoy eating the cake and
enjoy RPJ as well.

The Bible reports that the early Christians "ate their meat
with gladness."[13] Can I do that? If my heart condemns me
within, I know I'm virtually swapping that puny piece of cake
for RPJ afterward. What a bad deal! Other verses in Romans
14 advise us, "Happy is he who does not condemn himself in
what he approves,"[14] and "Each one should be fully convinced in his own mind."[15]

Romans 14 goes on to explain that we shouldn't allow any
freedom we enjoy to become an "occasion for the flesh," or to
cause someone watching us to "stumble." If you are a spiritual person, chances are that someone *is* watching you—to see
whether your beliefs make a difference in your life. Regardless of what is "legal" for us, at times we must choose re-
straint and personal denial. If we want to experience RPJ, we
have to accept that *we have a limited liberty.*

Once we have begun the spiritual journey to freedom from
private obsessions, our very real freedom is restricted by those
who observe our activities, by our confidants or partners, by
our conscience, by the Spirit of God within us. We can't

---

12. Emphasis added.
13. See Acts 2:46.
14. Verse 22.
15. Verse 5, NIV.

afford to disregard all of these and plunge headlong back into our obsessive behavior. Instead, our liberty must be *regulated from within*—and driven by our desire to "inherit the kingdom."

In each situation, therefore, we must ask ourselves:

Can I listen to this joke and not be affected?

Can I volunteer for this project and not be sucked in?

Can I honestly do what it takes to please this person and maintain my self-respect?

Can I do what I want to do . . . and still have RPJ?

MYSTERIES OF THE KINGDOM

I've experienced the incomparable value of kingdom living here on earth. I've received the treasure of his guilt-free, worry-free, joyful way of life. It's wonderful; I don't want to live any other way.

Why, then, do people act in ways that forfeit RPJ? Partly because they don't know what they're doing. In a way, this wonderful secret of RPJ seems "hidden"; it's not self-evident or obvious to the casual onlooker. We only find the kingdom by seeking it.

Jesus said as much. He compared the kingdom to a "treasure hidden in the field" which someone must "sell all" to buy. He also compares it to a "pearl of great value" that is worth giving up everything else to own.[16] And he refers to both these analogies as "mysteries of the kingdom."[17]

What he is really saying is, "How much is my kingdom worth to you? It should be worth everything!"

So let's decide to "trade up"! Make the choice to STOP, LOOK, LISTEN—and surrender your compulsive behavior now. Because your addiction is private, maybe no one will see the change. But *inside* you'll be developing a treasured feeling of peace, of "rightness," and of joy.

Hope is a great motivator. And the hope for a renewed sense of righteousness (to replace guilt), peace (in stressful times), and joy (in place of worry) is potent enough to carry

---

16. Matthew 13:44–46.
17. Verse 11.

us through our times of temptation. It can prevent us from reverting back to our cover-up behavior.

Like the manna in the wilderness of Moses,[18] RPJ. can only be collected "one day at a time." Fortunately, however, it is available on a daily basis. So don't worry about tomorrow. Seize the day and rejoice! The kingdom of God—and its righteousness, peace, and joy—is yours for the seeking.

---

18. See Exodus 16:35.

9

reparenting
yourself

overcoming past damage

- "My Mother always said I was lazy. And I guess she was right, because look at this messy house!"
- "If you'd been raised on pasta and rewarded with sweets, you'd know why I'm so compulsive about food."
- "Ever since I was molested as a child, I've been sort of mixed up about sex."
- "My dad left when I was eight. And at about that same time I seemed to develop this bad temper. 'Latent hostility,' I guess the shrinks would call it."

There is no escaping the fact that our parents play an enormous and continuing role in our lives, even if they are no longer living. No matter how close or distant our relationship to them, mothers and fathers (or their substitutes) mold us from day one, through what they say and what they do. Unless we have made a conscious effort to break away from their influence, we invariably view ourselves through our parents' eyes, and we frequently speak to ourselves with our parents' words. And we often identify ourselves with the labels our parents have placed upon us.

All our past experiences have contributed to making us what we are today—whether good or bad. In many ways, looking at the past can do a lot to explain the way we think, act, feel. But although memories can give us insight, they

don't give us an excuse. The past doesn't have to hold us
captive. With God's able assistance, we can reprogram ourselves with right, positive thinking—even redoing past damage inflicted on us by our parents. Before we look at some
"how to" specifics, however, let's look at some unhealthy
ways of looking into our personal past:

"THEY DONE ME WRONG!"—
THE TRAP OF RESENTMENT

Statistics tell us that 94 percent of Americans come from
so-called "dysfunctional families"—clinically described as
"any family systems not fulfilling their role as a successfully
functioning family." So does that mean that 94 percent of us
are justified in being weird, difficult, unpleasant, or self-
destructive?

Just about everyone has some sort of an alibi. But is living
with a litany of excuses really satisfying? Instead, let's allow
our family members to bear the burden of what they've done
wrong in the past. Their choices are their responsibility. It's
up to us to bear the responsibility for the way we are *today*. If
I choose to stay the way "they" made me, I am the one responsible for what goes wrong.

> Those who did me wrong in the past
> are responsible for the past.
> I am responsible for the present.

So let's not waste any more time hating our past or resent-
ing the people in it. No matter how bad it was, it served a
purpose. It gave us the raw material to become the men and
women God intended us to be. After all, when the apostle
Paul said, "*All things* work together for good to them that love
God,"[1] he wasn't just talking about the good experiences, the
happy times, the pleasant events. Every incident we've ever

---

1. Romans 8:28, KJV, emphasis added.

encountered—absurd, appalling, even awful—can contribute to our lives for our ultimate good.

Besides, when we consciously hold a resentment, refusing to forgive, we are volunteering to give the people who hurt us further control over our lives. This means we give them the power to hurt us again and again. Someone has said,

> **When you hold resentments,**
> **you are allowing**
> **those who wronged you**
> **to live inside your head, rent-free!**

"I MUST DIAGNOSE WHAT HAPPENED"— THE TRAP OF OVERANALYSIS

And while we're on the subject of "the past," let's note that it's not necessary to understand the past completely in order to put it in its place. Many types of therapy involve the imaginative reenactment or reliving of past traumas. Such perilous "inner journeys" can supposedly even date back to the womb, a process sometimes identified with "primal scream" therapy.

I believe such therapies hold the potential for great harm. Too often, they drag the subject back through all sorts of past garbage and abuses. As if the victims weren't traumatized enough back then, now they are forced to reexperience all sorts of painful experiences in order to be "free." But even when such therapies don't cause damage in themselves, I believe they are largely a waste of time.

I would include such therapies under what the Bible termed "vain . . . imaginations."[2] It is important to realize that *imagination* is very different from *revelation*. Imagination is something willfully conjured up—even forced. Revelation from God's Spirit gently surfaces at the proper time and brings with

---

2. Rom. 1:21. See also Psalms 2:1 and Acts 4:25.
3. Isaiah 9:60

it a generous dose of healing grace. God is our "Wonderful Counselor"[3]—we should let him guide the process of dealing with our past. Subjecting ourselves to destructive and disruptive manmade therapies often summons up more confusion than healing.

Looking at the past is helpful, even necessary, as part of the process of recovering from hidden addictions. But spending significant time in the past through self-analysis or reenactment therapies is quite another matter.

In *Hooked on Life*, a book on recovery from addictive behavior, authors Steve Arterburn and Tim Timmons compare our consideration of the past to looking in a rear-view mirror:

> When we are driving, reality is what we see approaching us. We must face forward, ready to respond to whatever might be ahead. But drivers need to maintain perspective and know what is approaching from the rear: hence a small rear-view mirror is attached to the windshield. Drivers with a rearview mirror as large as the windshield would have little chance of a safe trip. Don't allow the view of the rear to completely block out the approaching reality.[4]

I'd like to encourage you *not* to volunteer for another extensive archaeological dig into your past. Major digs are costly, time consuming, and can be dangerous. (Just ask Indiana Jones!) Let's agree not to spend the next few years of our lives delving into yesterday. That particular ditch has no visible bottom—and we may pick up an analysis addiction along the way.

Why things happened to us in the past is not as important as *how* we can alter their effect on the present. Digging up and dissecting the roots of the "family tree" can torment us forever if we don't develop a plan for recovery.

---

4. Steve Arterburn and Tim Timmons, *Hooked on Life* (Nashville: Thomas Nelson, 1985), 124.

FINDING AN ALTERNATE ROAD

So, on to the present! Once we've jettisoned the baggage of resentful thinking and avoided the treacherous "I must reexperience it" philosophy, it's time we set out on a new course, determined to repair parenting damage in our lives and make the most of our future. But, as someone said, "A driving ambition is of little use if you are on the wrong road!" David Viscott, in his book, *Risking*, encourages us:

> No one can make you change,
> No one can stop you from changing.
> No one really knows how
> you must change — not even you —
> until you start.[5]

HOW PARENTING CONTRIBUTES
TO OUR PRIVATE OBSESSIONS

Quite a few of our private obsessions feed on our perceived lack of love. We are often deeply wounded by the love we felt we never received, but were entitled to. (Note the emphasis here on "felt." It's the *perception* that makes the difference here, not the reality.) Trying somehow to compensate for past or present deprivations, we seek love and acceptance in work, relationships, possessions, appearances, or other distractions. Unfortunately, these activities simply cannot meet our deep longings.

Some of our compulsions, in addition, may reflect an ongoing effort to please our parents, long after that should be a dominant influence in our lives. We work hard, clean hard, study hard—still hoping to be the "good little girl" (or boy) our parents would approve.

---

5. David Viscott, *Risking* (New York: Pocket Books, 1988).

Or maybe we act compulsively because we are subconsciously rebelling against our parents. We gamble or smoke or overeat because our parents didn't approve of such actions and we're determined (perhaps subconsciously) that they "won't tell me what to do."

Well, friends, guess what? Unless you're under eighteen and living at home, it's too late! It's too late to be a "Daddy's little darling," too late to be a "good little girl," too late to be a "rebel without a cause."

If your parent(s) are still living, it may not be too late to show them forgiveness and respect, to talk out differences and heal strained relationships. But it is too late to redo what has happened. No matter what our addictive behavior, we will never be able to make up for what our parents did or failed to do when we were children.

What I'm talking about, therefore, is our tendency to indulge in negative behavior because of old, past childhood issues. That's the kind of behavior we are trying to overcome through the reparenting process.

OPT OUT OF THE BLAME GAME!

Forgiveness is the primary solvent for removing and erasing the effects of the past. We talked about this in the LOOK chapter—understanding the impact others have made in our lives and then, if necessary, forgiving the negative impact was part of the process of taking a personal inventory.

But bear in mind that this effort may not be the last, final time you'll need to forgive those people. Some hurts have to be forgiven time after time, again and again—and still their pain recurs. But if you consciously voice your forgiveness whenever you are reminded of a painful experience, I guarantee the forgiveness will "take hold" in your life—you will gradually become free of the power those people have over you.

Opting for forgiveness means refusing to play the blame game anymore. Stop asking the great cop-out question: "Whose fault is it that I'm this way?" Don't blame yourself, but take responsibility for yourself as of now. The blame goes beyond your grandparents anyway, all the way back to that notorious buck-passing trio—Adam, Eve, and the serpent!

Sometimes it is helpful to remember that our parents had problems of their own that may have shaped the way they reared us. They may have grown up in unenlightened times and places, for example, where parenting was summed up in the phrase, "Children are to be seen and not heard" or "Spare the rod and spoil the child" (interpreted as "lay that rod on hard!"). Many of them were abused, and others were ignored.

Adult Children of Alcoholics must learn to understand that no parent, past, present or future, intentionally becomes an alcoholic. Similarly, very few parents set about to reject their children—or neglect them—or die "on purpose" to "abandon" them. Most of our mothers and fathers did the best they could, all the while knowing deep inside that it really wasn't enough.

The first step of reparenting, therefore, is to opt out of the blame game. Repeat outloud to yourself: "My parents loved me the best they were able." Then realize that it's OK if you feel cheated. In spite of their well-intentioned efforts, you probably *were* short-changed, one way or another. It's a good thing God is around to help even out the rough spots that occur in everyone's childhood.

THE GAP THEORY

"God couldn't be everywhere, so he created mothers," the flowery motto goes. Not true. Not one of our mothers was ever capable of filling the God-gap in our lives. Many men and women feel cheated by insufficient parenting. A gap exists between the parenting they needed and what they got. We've already come to see that things, people, and experiences won't fill it. Only God can fill up that loveless cavity that aches so painfully in the midst of our daily lives.

The deep emptiness we feel is really in the human spirit. And it must be satisfied in order for us to feel whole and complete. The body is governed by our willpower. The soul is governed by our intellect, will, and emotions (and, by the way, we haven't done so well in any of those departments). But the spirit is to be ruled by faith, and it's up to God to

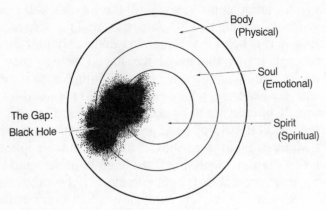

Figure 5 — The Gap

supply what we need in this vital and much-neglected area. Quality recovery from addiction will involve emotional and physical discipline, yes. But it really takes hold as healing comes to the root of our innermost spirits.

God the Father is the only one capable of loving us unconditionally. And he is able to do what our parents were not able to do. God loves us with a healthy love, a perfect love. He will reveal it to us in ways that only we can fully understand and appreciate. And God's revelation of his love is always more wonderful than we could ask or think possible.

So the second step of reparenting, after you forgive your parents for their failures, is to pray, "Father in heaven, fill the gap between the love I've received and the love I need with your love for me." And then let God love you, his way, today!

ERASE YOUR TAPES

Once you've let go of your resentment and asked God to fill in the gaps in your parenting, you can begin the process of "reprogramming" yourself for healthy behavior. With God's help, it is both possible and appropriate to "reparent" ourselves with love, gentleness, and understanding. To begin with, you must make a conscious decision not to listen to those past "tapes," recorded in earlier days, that forever play in your head:

- "You're a lazy slob! You'll never amount to anything!"
- "You're built just like your Aunt Matilda, and you know how fat she is. . . ."
- "With all your potential, you should be doing a lot better. You just don't try!"
- "All you ever do is look in that mirror! How conceited can you get?"
- "If you're so bored, go make yourself a sandwich. Just don't bother me. I'm busy."

When you hear these kinds of words in your head or think these thoughts, stop yourself. Remind yourself that statements like that aren't true, they aren't kind, they aren't appropriate, they aren't fair. It really is possible to erase those old tapes and make kinder, gentler ones!

GROWING YOURSELF UP AGAIN

The actual process of reparenting yourself is, basically, the act of doing for yourself what a good parent would or should do:

- Building your self-confidence.
- Providing for you.
- Protecting you.
- Disciplining you.
- Affirming your strengths.
- Pointing you toward your heavenly Father.

It involves deliberately saying "yes" to yourself—making new, affirmative "tapes" that tell you:

- "Yes, it's OK for you to feel these emotions now—and anyway, they will pass."
- "Yes! You deserve to have your needs met."
- "Yes, you are a lovely, caring person. You do a lot of nice things for other people."
- "Yes, you look really nice today."
- "Yes! I'm proud of you!"
- (add your own) "Yes, _____."
- "Yes, _____."

It's also a process of learning to tell yourself no about harmful activities:

- "No, you can't have this affair; I won't let you!"
- "No, you know how crazy you get when you drink."
- "No! You look so attractive when you're thin, I don't want you to sacrifice your looks for some food you don't really need."
- "No, don't spend the money. You'll regret it later."
- "No, don't call him. Let him call you this time, and you'll be more assured that he really cares."
- "No, you're overdoing it now."
- "No, don't register for that guilt trip!"
- (add your own) "No, _____."
- "No, _____."

As we both commend ourselves and call ourselves up short, as any good parent would do, we begin to carve out new habit patterns to replace the old ruts. And when we do that, we are "loving" ourselves the way God does—with acceptance, forgiveness, and desire for our personal best. After all, if we can't love ourselves, we can never properly love our "neighbor as ourselves."[6]

REMEMBER WHOSE CHILD YOU REALLY ARE!

Throughout the whole process of reparenting yourself, determine to:

> **View your biological parents
> simply as the
> instruments of your existence.**

Bear it well in mind: your mother and dad were used to produce you, but you were God's idea! If the Bible is true, children are his "conception," and not really the parents'.

---

6. See Matthew 5:43.

How do you think it happened? *You*, I mean! Do you imagine that years ago your dad winked at your mom and said, "Let's go upstairs and make a little Margaret tonight!" No way! Maybe dad wasn't thinking about Margaret . . . but Somebody else definitely was. When you look at it God's way, there are no illegitimate children. They all belong to him.

Our primary parent is our heavenly Father. And he can help us parent ourselves successfully by teaching us about his own unconditional love for us. So make up your mind to treat yourself as well as he treats you! Let me share with you how I learned to do just that with one of my own private obsessions.

REPARENTING LEE

"Idle hands are the devil's playground" was ingrained in me by my mother at a very early age. It took me years to realize that this message is not necessarily true. Meanwhile, my acute fear of becoming "a lazy good-for-nothing" spurred me on to become a practicing workaholic.

My father's alcoholism no doubt contributed to my compulsiveness. His drunken stupors incapacitated him; he could accomplish little or nothing. In reaction I promised myself, over and over: "I'm going to *do* something, make something out of myself!" I required myself to pursue many valuable accomplishments—working so hard that my projects became far more important than people. Meanwhile, I became convinced that my value was somehow wrapped up in what I did, not in who I was. I worked far too hard and cared far too little about those around me.

Then, as God began to mend my past hurts, I began to get the picture. I began to understand the truth that "Mother is always right" and "Father knows best" are myths! (If you're an honest parent, you'll agree with that!)

Eventually I came to realize that I needed to reprogram my tapes. Idle hands are not the devil's playground; they are just resting! Now I know my job is to work hard, *and* to play hard. Taking time—no, *making time* for leisure is not only legal, but necessary.

Christ calls to us, "Come unto me . . . and I will give you rest."[7] As a workaholic, I've had to hear that message addressed to me: "Come unto me *now* . . . and I will teach you *how* to rest."

Today, I even let people catch me resting once in awhile! I am learning to stop and smell the roses.

What about you? What did your parents say to you that drives you obsessively even today? What kind of stories are your "old tapes" telling you? I suggest you rewind them and start them over. Rerecord the following message about a Heavenly Parent who *is* always right, and who *does* know best!

> We know how much God loves us because we have felt his love and because we believe him when he tells us that he loves us dearly. . . .
>
> We need have no fear of someone who loves us perfectly; his perfect love for us eliminates all dread of what he might do to us. If we are afraid, it is for fear of what he might do to us, and shows that we are not fully convinced that he really loves us. So you see, our love for him comes as a result of his loving us first. . . .
>
> And God himself has said that one must love not only God, but his brother too.[8]

---

7. Matthew 11:28, KJV.
8. First John 4:16–21, TLB.

after
the magnificent obsession

Now that you've nearly finished reading this book, I hope you've discovered some personal insights for yourself—insights that shed bright beams of light on the private obsessions that may be shadowing your life. If that's the case, perhaps it has given you the extra push you needed to change things for the better. Maybe taking the time to consider obsessive behavior has, as the psalmist put it, allowed you to see your "secret sins in the light of [God's] presence."[1] And maybe you've learned to STOP, LOOK, and LISTEN your way to freedom:

STOP—

- to evaluate and admit your powerlessness.
- to change a potentially harmful habit pattern.
- to develop your spiritual life with Christ, your Higher Power.

LOOK—

- beyond the action and thought to consider whether past pain is contributing to present behavior?
- behind, to clear the past with forgiveness.
- ahead, to develop a disciplined life.

LISTEN—

- to your conscience and instincts.
- to supportive friends with whom you've been honest about your behavior.
- to the Spirit of God who desires to lead you into his kingdom of righteousness, peace, and joy.

---

1. Psalms 90:8.

TWO STEPS FORWARD, ONE STEP BACK

It's important to realize, however, that the road to freedom is seldom a straight, even one. We can seek the kingdom of God first. We can STOP, LOOK, and LISTEN. We can rerecord our parenting tapes. Yet none of these efforts guarantees we'll never again fall back into our old obsessive ways. Occasionally we may get waylaid—bingeing on our old, addictive behavior. After months of self-control, we find ourselves cleaning out the malls, camping out in front of the TV, plowing through the coupons again—and furious with ourselves.

"Relapse," the AA program calls it. However you term it, it's real. It happens to most people at least once. That's why it's imperative to keep in mind constantly that we're dealing with the God of new beginnings.

Be assured that failing doesn't make you a failure. You just blew it, that's all! And you can be sure that now that you've committed yourself to facing up to the problem, you will sense an inner conviction that is different from condemnation or guilt. This conviction will give you determination, wooing you back to the straight and narrow. You'll want to try again, and try harder than before. Do it! STOP, LOOK, LISTEN. And once again, start moving toward freedom. And remember:

```
          The task ahead of us
            is never as great
        as the Power behind us!
```

The Argentine pastor Dr. Juan Carlos Ortiz put it this way: "We must give God our willpower; he will give us the power steering." Yes, thank God, we don't have to deal with our problems alone. Christianity is not a do-it-yourself religion. When I find myself complaining, "but I can't . . . ," I remember the apostle Paul's words, "I *can* do all things through [Christ] who strengthens me."[2]

---

2. Philippians 4:13, emphasis added.

But that same victorious apostle Paul also penned, "For that which I am doing, I do not understand; for I am not practicing what I would like to do, but I am doing the very thing I hate."[3] Even Paul did not always bat in the most victorious league. But he was forever reaching for the principles that would enable him to keep practicing—and moving toward victory.

STAY CLOSE TO THE DRIVER

As I have already indicated, I believe the numerous habit patterns we've talked about are ultimately of spiritual origin and must be dealt with through the application of spiritual principles. As I've also indicated, this doesn't necessarily mean that they relate directly to our eternal salvation.

But in a way, worrying about "ultimate destinations" is a little beside the point. Someone has likened the spiritual life to a dozen Christians riding in the back of a pickup truck. Some of them believe the tailgate is locked; others think it's open. When it comes to our compulsions, it's not essential that we know the answer to "how far we may fall." Why take the chance of falling off the truck by leaning out the back or straddling the side? Let's choose to huddle together, hold on tight, and ride as close to the Driver as possible!

In the meantime, let's also become "ruthless" in rooting out unhealthy distractions from our lives. Self-control is not a "gift" from God." It is a "fruit" of Spirit-filled living, and it is our responsibility to cultivate its growth.[4] We need to bite the proverbial bullet of discipline and no longer rationalize any temporary giving in to our old ways.

It's wise to bear in mind that God never tempts anyone.[5] We arrange our own temptation scenarios, thank you. We set ourselves up to charge another purchase, adopt another pet, meet another man, pack another storage box, or whatever it is that we're habitually apt to do. It is our job, therefore, to continuously protect ourselves from what "triggers"

---

3. Romans 7:15.
4. Galatians 5:23.
5. James 1:13.

obsessive behavior in us; we've got to avoid the old cues and ask God's help in passing by the ones we cannot avoid.

We also need to take a hard look at our private obsessions and see them for what they really are. Each kind of hidden addiction affects our lives in a different way. Yet they are all alike in that they become controlling elements in our lives— taking the place of God. And the Bible has a very specific word for putting anything in God's place: *idolatry.*

"Idolatry? You've got to be kidding! I don't pray to idols!" you may protest. No, you probably don't. Yet when you look outward or inward to things or people or experiences in order to find personal satisfaction, you *aren't* looking in the right direction—toward heaven. No wonder you can't find the satisfaction you want.

MOVE FROM SELF-INDULGENCE TO SELF-DENIAL

And by now, I hope we've begun to see the advantage of deny-ing ourselves the luxury of self-centeredness. Becoming "others-centered" can release us from our indulgent compulsions.

```
The recovery process
        carries us
     from hurting
        to healing
   to helping others.
```

Once we are actively involved in our recovery process, we'll find honesty with others a natural outcome. As Shakespeare once said, "To thine own self be true, and it must follow, as the night the day, thou canst not then be false to any man."[6] As we share our faults and listen to the problems of others, perhaps we can even assist them to begin their own process of recovery. Looking "on the things of others"[7] is one sure way to get us out of the overanalysis rut!

6. Hamlet, iii.580.
7. Philippians 2:4.

For example, studying addictive behaviors may have reminded you of a friend or loved one who is suffering, unaware that help is available. Depending on what your friend's problem is, you may want to ask yourself first: "Am I enabling these problems in some way? Am I excusing them? Am I a part of the problem or the solution?" If the addiction is serious enough to be affecting others as well, you'll want to talk it over with your friend. Pray specifically that God will give you wisdom and prepare her (or his) heart for anything you may have to say.

As we reach out to others, however, it's important to keep our motivations in mind. Because compulsive people are such great rationalizers and so adept at trading one private obsession for another, we need to keep an eye on what we're doing. For instance, are you really reaching out, or are you just distracting yourself from your own weaknesses?

Our knowledge of addictive behavior can help set ourselves and others free. But it neither gives us *license to justify* nor ordains us *legalists to judge.* At best, we are all "fellow strugglers."

HAVE A SWAP MEET

Now that we're aware of our weaknesses, we won't be so willing to swap and trade down. An old adage goes, "Good is the enemy of the *best.*" No more are we willing to trade in RPJ for the temporary highs and lows of addictive behavior. If there's any trading to be done, we're going to trade in the behavior we thought was "not so bad" and buy "the best" with it—sensing God's righteousness, peace and joy.

When we become spiritually alive through our new life in Christ, we become a little like Lazarus, who was raised from physical death by Jesus. He came forth from the grave alive, but he was still bound in grave cloths. "Unbind him and set him free," the Lord instructed his friends. I believe Jesus would say the very same thing concerning our private obsessions. As we choose to become alive in the Spirit, we need to be free from anything that binds us, or hinders our movement, or limits our energy and effectiveness. "If the Son sets you free, you will be free indeed."[8]

---

8. John 8:36, NIV.

You know, you *can* make it, along with me, *one day at a time*. Big promises and proclamations are unnecessary. As the old hymn, "Great Is Thy Faithfulness" promises, God gives "strength for today and bright hope for tomorrow!"[8] My heartfelt prayer is that, as you increase your awareness of private obsessions in your life, you will be led to a wonderful new life of strength and bright hope.

Just remember—*any* habit which hinders the quality of our lives and over which we must confess powerlessness, must be eliminated. That means "casting down . . . every lofty thing that exalts itself against the knowledge of God, and bringing every thought into captivity to the obedience of Christ."[9]

As Oswald Chambers said so well in his classic book *My Utmost for His Highest*,

> The first thing to do in examining the power that dominates me is to take hold of the unwelcome fact that I am responsible for being thus dominated. Yield in childhood to selfishness, and you will find it the most enchaining tyranny on earth. "His servants ye are to whom ye obey" [Rom. 6:16]. You must yield yourself in utter humiliation to the only one who can break the dominating power viz., the Lord Jesus Christ—"He hath anointed me . . . to preach deliverance to all captives."[10]

With this in mind, the only obsession we want to permit into our lives is the quest for the fullness of the kingdom of God within.

And what a Magnificent Obsession that is!

---

9. Thomas O. Chisholm. Copyright 1923. Renewal 1951 by Hope Publishing Company, Carol Stream, Il 60188. All Rights Reserved. Used by Permission.

10. 2 Corinthians 10:5.

11. Oswald Chambers, *My Utmost for His Highest* (New York: Dodd, Mead, 1935), 74.

recommended reading

Hemfelt, Robert, Frank Minirth, Paul Meyer, and Sharon Sneed. *Love Hunger: Recovery for Food Codependence.* Nashville: Thomas Nelson, 1990.

Arterburn, Stephen. *Toxic Faith.* Nashville: Thomas Nelson, 1991.

Foster, Richard. *Celebration of Discipline.* San Francisco: Harper & Row, 1978.

LeSourd, Sandra. *The Compulsive Woman.* Old Tappan, NJ: Chosen, 1987.

Minirth, Frank and Paul Meier. *Food Addiction.* Nashville: Thomas Nelson, 1990.

Bartosch, Bob and Pauline Bartosch. *Freed.* La Habra, CA: Overcomers Outreach, 1985.

Lewis, C. S. *Mere Christianity.* New York: Macmillan, 1952.

Ellis, Alfred. *One-Way Relationships.* Nashville: Thomas Nelson, 1990.

Augustine Fellowship, The. *Sex and Love Addicts Anonymous.* Boston: Fellowship Wide Services, 1986.

Hansel, Tim. *When I Relax I Feel Guilty.* Elgin, IL: David C. Cook, 1987.

Hart, Archibald D. *Healing Life's Hidden Addictions.* Ann Arbor, MI: Servant Publications, 1990.

Miller, Keith. *Hope in the Fast Lane: A New Look at Faith in a Compulsive World.* San Francisco, Harper & Row, 1987.

W., Claire. *"God, Help Me Stop.* San Diego: Books West, 1982.

organizations and support groups

NATIONAL LISTINGS OF SUPPORT GROUPS

Overcomers Outreach (Christian Support Groups)
    2290 West Whittier Boulevard,
    Suite D
    La Habra, CA 90631
    (213) 697-3994

National Self-Help Clearinghouse
    33 West 42nd St.
    New York, NY 10036
    (Send stamped, self-addressed envelope
      for information)

HELP FOR SPECIFIC ADDICTION PROBLEMS

ALCOHOL

Alcoholics Victorious (Christian Help)
    P.O. Box 10364
    Portland, OR 97232
    (503) 245-9629

Christian Alcoholics Rehabilitation Association
    FOA Road
    Pocahontas, MI 39072

Alcoholics Anonymous
    468 Park Avenue South
    New York, NY 10016
    (212) 686-1100

DRUG ABUSE

Substance Abusers Victorious (Christian Support Groups)
One Cascade Plaza
Akron, OH 44308

Narcotics Anonymous
P.O. Box 9999
Van Nuys, CA 91409
(818) 780-3951

COMPULSIVE EATING

Overeaters Anonymous
2190 199th Street
Torrance, CA 90504
(213) 657-6252

GAMBLING

Gamblers Anonymous
P.O. Box 17173
Los Angeles, CA 90017
(213) 386-8789

SEX ABUSE

Sexaholics Anonymous
P.O. Box 300
Simi Valley, CA 93062

New Life Treatment Centers, Inc.
(800) 227-LIFE,
(800) 332-TEEN

SHOPAHOLICS

Debtors Anonymous
Box 20322
New York, NY 10025

Shopaholics, Limited
(212) 675-4342